P9-BYZ-268

Better Sentence-Writing In 30 Minutes a Day

By
Dianna Campbell

CAREER PRESS
3 Tice Road
P.O. Box 687
Franklin Lakes, NJ 07417
1-800-CAREER-1
201-848-0310 (outside U.S.)
FAX: 201-848-1727

BETTER SENTENCE-WRITING IN 30 MINUTES A DAY
ISBN 1-56414-203-5, $8.99
Cover design by The Visual Group
Printed in the U.S.A. by Book-mart Press

To order this title by mail, please include price as noted above, $2.50 handling per order, and $1.00 for each book ordered. Send to: Career Press, Inc., 3 Tice Road, P.O. Box 687, Franklin Lakes, NJ 07417.

Or call toll-free 1-800-CAREER-1 (Canada: 201-848-0310) to order using VISA or MasterCard, or for further information on books from Career Press.

Library of Congress Cataloging-in-Publication Data

Campbell, Dianna S., 1949-
  Better sentence-writing in 30 minutes a day / by Dianna Campbell.
    p.   cm.
  Includes bibliographical references and index.
  ISBN 1-56414-203-5 (paper)
  1. English language--Sentences. 2. English language--Rhetoric.
  I. Title.
PE1441.C27   1995
  428.2--dc20   95-22181
                                                              CIP

Contents

i

Preface

Better Sentence-Writing In 30 Minutes a Day is a workbook for students who have thought seriously about how important it is to improve the technical aspects of their writing. Learning to write well is nothing less than acquiring the power to succeed—in school and in the world that lies beyond school. Developing solid writing skills is not a matter of luck; it's a matter of hard work and practice.

This book features a basic sentence-combining approach, which means that the emphasis is not merely on learning to avoid errors, but also on learning to create good sentences with variety and style. The book also features:

- Clear discussions of rules and strategies for good writing.

- Concise explanations with a minimum of grammatical terms.

- An abundant variety of exercises, from filling-in-the-blank for purposes of identifying the parts of speech to combining short sentences into longer and more graceful combinations.

- An answer key at the end of the book to allow students to work at their own pace and check their work as they go.

Better Sentence-Writing

Students learn best when they are actively engaged in the learning process. They appreciate exercises that teach them the writing skills they need and entertain or inform them at the same time. That is why this book uses a variety of interesting topics in the exercises. Similarly, the instructional material here is brief, but extensive examples and illustrations are provided.

Using *Better Sentence-Writing In 30 Minutes a Day* will help students become skillful and confident writers.

Dianna Campbell

Chapter 1

Introduction to Sentence Structure

1.1 Basic Clause Patterns

Some college students can define a sentence, and some can't, but no doubt you know a sentence when you see one. Read the following choices and circle the letter of the one that is a sentence.

(a) Noses entire people's throughout grow lives their.

(b) Their grow lives throughout people's noses entire

(c) Grow lives their people's entire throughout noses.

(d) People's noses grow throughout their entire lives.

Each of the four sentences contains the same words, but only one makes *sense*—(d). Sequence (d) makes sense because the words in it are arranged in the form of a sentence. Your ability to recognize the sentence shows how natural the sentence pattern is and how much intuitive language skill you already have.

1

Better Sentence-Writing

Simple Sentences—Those with One Clause

In order to make good sentences and avoid making errors, we need to develop a basic working definition of a sentence. Sentences are made up of *clauses*—sometimes one clause, sometimes more than one. This chapter focuses on *simple sentences*—those that contain one clause. Later, you'll work with sentences that contain more than one clause.

A clause is a subject plus a predicate. The *subject* of a clause names something, such as a person, object, place, or idea. The subject is usually one or more nouns or pronouns. The subject might also be a noun substitute.

The *predicate* makes a statement about the subject by telling something about it. The predicate tells one of two things about the subject: It tells that the subject is performing an action, or it states the condition of the subject.

Finding Verbs in Clauses

The easiest way to analyze a clause is to look first at the predicate. The most important part of the predicate is the verb.

1. Action Verbs—Visible and Invisible

You probably know that most verbs show some kind of action. Sometimes this is *visible action*, as in *she swims* or *they kissed.* At other times, it is invisible action, as in *he forgot* or *we decided.*

The verb in our original example sentence shows visible action. Draw a line beneath the verb and write *v* above it.

People's noses grow throughout their entire lives.

If you identified *grow,* you're correct. That's the word that shows the visible action of the subject. What's the subject doing? In this sentence, it's growing.

2. Linking Verbs

Other verbs, such as is and *seem,* don't show an action; instead, they show a subject to be in a certain *condition* or state of being. They do this by *linking* the subject to a word or words in the predicate. These verbs are *linking verbs.* Let's look at two example sentences:

The woman is an intern.

The students seem confident.

In these sentences, the woman and the students are not performing actions, but they are in a state of being or a condition. We might say that, in the first case, the woman is in the state of being an intern and, in the second case, the students are in the condition of being confident.

There are many linking verbs, such as additional tenses of the verb *to be (am, are, was, were, will be, has been, have been, had been,* and others) and various forms of the verbs *appear, become, feel, look, smell, sound,* and *taste.*

3. The Role of Context

Some verbs are action verbs in one context and linking verbs in another. In sentence (a), is the italicized verb describing an action or a condition?

(a) I *smelled* the familiar fragrance of Chanel No. 5 in the living room.

In (a), the verb from *smelled* is describing an action, the action of the subject (I) smelling. Now notice the very different meaning of the same word in sentence (b).

(b) The rotten chicken *smelled* terrible.

In (b), the subject *(chicken),* is *not* performing an action. The verb in (b) shows that the chicken is in a certain condition—the condition of smelling bad.

Finding Subjects in Clauses

Let's return again to our original example sentence:

People's noses grow throughout their entire lives.

To find the subject, simply ask yourself, "What grows?" *Noses*. The word *noses* is the *simple subject* or the *key word* within the complete subject. The complete subject of any sentence is the simple subject or key word plus all the modifiers attached to it.

Throughout our work with clauses, we'll focus on the key word or words within the complete subject because that's what is most directly tied to the predicate. A key word is what the predicate makes a statement about. And, in the present tense, it's the simple subject with which the verb must agree.

Finding Elements That Complete the Verb

In the sentence *People's noses grow throughout their entire lives*, nothing is needed to complete the verb *grow*. Even though four words follow *grow* in the sentence, those words are not needed for sentence structure. They're needed for the writer's meaning, but not for completing the clause. The subject and verb *(noses grow)* make a certain kind of sense and give a feeling of completeness.

But there are other verbs that, by themselves, cannot make a complete structure with a subject. Consider these subject and verb combinations:

they desire

she said

the tree was

people need

Bill kissed

tourists want

These sets leave you hanging, wondering: They desire what? She said what? Bill kissed whom? In each case, the verb needs a word or words to complete its meaning. The words that do this job in the predicate of a clause are called *complements* and *objects*. We'll look at their basic types.

1. Subject Complements

One important kind of complement is the subject complement, which follows a linking verb. A subject complement is a noun, pronoun, adjective, or adverb of place that follows a verb in a clause. Here are some sentences in which the subject complements are underlined:

Martha Aliaga is a superb <u>math teacher.</u>

The subject complement answers the question, "Martha Aliaga is what?"

The juniors are our <u>representatives</u> on the committee.

The subject complement answers the question, "The juniors are what?"

James feels <u>wonderful.</u>

The subject complement answers the question, "James feels how?"

2. Direct and Indirect Objects

Direct Objects Linking verbs are not the only kind of verb that needs completion. Another type of verb that needs completion is a kind of action verb called the *transitive verb*. This is a verb that carries or transfers action from the subject before the verb to the object after the verb.

The words that complete the meaning of transitive verbs are called *direct objects*. They follow action verbs and answer the

Better Sentence-Writing

question "What?" or "Whom?" A good example is *I need you.* *You* is the direct object of the verb *need.*

Do all sentences with action verbs have direct objects? Let's return to the first sentence we considered: *People's noses grow throughout their entire lives.* This sentence has an action verb, but it doesn't have an object. The verb *grow* doesn't need one; *noses grow* has a sense of completeness. Although *grow* shows action, here it is not a transitive verb; it's an *intransitive verb.* It does not move or transport action from the subject to the object. So some action verbs are intransitive, and all linking verbs are intransitive.

So far, we've only looked at linking verbs, because linking verbs are the only kind that are followed by subject complements. In these next sentences, we'll see only action verbs, because action verbs are the kind that take direct objects. We'll label the direct object *do* and underline it:

do
We passed <u>the collection basket</u>.
The direct object answers the question, "We passed what?"

do
Frank paid the <u>money</u>.

The direct object answers the question, "Frank paid what?"
One way to check if a word is a direct object is to try using it as the subject of a passive version of the same sentence. If it *is* a direct object, it will work as the subject. For example, the active sentence *We passed the collection basket* becomes the passive sentence *The collection basket was passed by us.*

If a sentence has a linking verb and a subject complement, you won't be able to transform it from active into passive. This transformation works only with sentences that contain direct objects.

Indirect Objects Sometimes the predicate of a clause also contains a word that is *indirectly* affected by the verb. This word is called the *indirect object*, and it comes before the direct

6

object. The indirect object tells to whom or for whom an action is done. We'll use *IO* as the abbreviation for indirect object.

io   do

We passed <u>the boy</u> the <u>collection basket</u>.

We passed what? The basket. To whom? To the boy.

io   do

Francie sent <u>Eduardo</u> the <u>money</u>.

Francie sent what? The money. For whom? For Eduardo.
If you are having difficulty keeping direct and indirect objects straight, reconsider the first sentence. Did we pass the boy from person to person? Or did we pass the collection basket? Which word is *directly* affected by the verb *passed?* It's *basket*—the direct object. The word *boy* is only *indirectly* affected, so it's the indirect object.

Some common verbs that are followed by both indirect and direct objects are the forms of *bring, buy, give, lend, offer, sell, send,* and *write.* Try writing a few simple sentences with these verbs, and you'll probably automatically create clauses with both indirect and direct objects.

3. Object Complements

Some direct objects need a little something extra. They themselves need to be completed by an *object complement.* This word clarifies the meaning of the verb in a sentence or makes the meaning richer. The object complement always follows a direct object, and it helps to complete a direct object by identifying or modifying it.

Object complements are often found in clauses with verbs such as *appoint, choose, consider, elect, make, name,* and *think.* These verbs have one thing in common: They all roughly mean to *make* or *consider.*

7

Better Sentence-Writing

We'll use *ob com* as our abbreviation. Here are some examples:

do ob com

We painted the <u>town</u> <u>red</u>.

Can you see how this sentence means roughly the same as "We *made* the town red"?

do   ob com

Gerald called his <u>mother</u> <u>a saint</u>.

This sentence is similar to "Gerald *considered* his mother a saint."

Like subject complements, object complements can be nouns or adjectives. Clauses with object complements don't occur as often as the other types of clauses we've examined.

Summary of Basic Clause Types

There are five basic types of clause.

1. subject + verb

s   v

Example: The children played.

2. subject + linking verb + subject complement

s   v   sub com

Example: You are beautiful.

3. subject + verb + direct object

s   v   do

Example: Roosevelt inspired everyone.

4. subject + verb + indirect object + direct object

s   v   io   do

Example: Samantha sold her friend an antique ruby ring.

5. subject + verb + direct object + object complement

s   v   do ob com

Example: Marvin called his lab partner a witch.

Exercise 1.1

In the following sentences, label the subject *s*, the verb *v*, the direct object *do*, the indirect object *io*, the subject complement *sub com*, and the object complement *ob com*.

1. His motive was mysterious.

2. I bought the suit.

3. The woman in the second row coughed.

4. Caroline gave Steven a choice.

5. The nectarines feel ripe.

A note on multiple parts: In the remaining exercises, you may find clauses with more than one key word in the subject or more than one verb, complement, or object. In the following sentences, use the blanks provided to identify the multiple parts that appear in italics:

1. *Rose, gray,* and *white* are her favorite colors.

   _____

2. He *loves* and *respects* her. _____

3. The little girl is *curious* and *spunky.* _____

4. I bought *fudge, cashews,* and a *newspaper.* _____

5. The architect gave her *clients* and the entire *audience* a real surprise. _____

6. The release of the movie made him *rich* and *famous.*

   _____

7. The decision *surprised Isaac* and angered *Anna.*

   _____ _____

Item 1 has three key words in the subject. Item 2 has two verbs. Item 3 has two subject complements. Item 4 has three direct objects. Item 5 has two indirect objects. Item 6 has two object complements. Item 7 has two verbs *(surprised* and *angered)* and two direct objects *(Isaac* and *Anna).*

Exercise 1.2

Label the parts of the following simple sentences, using *s* for subject, *v* for verb, *do* for direct object, *io* for indirect object, *sub com* for subject complement, and *ob com* for object complement. Remember: Find the verb first.

1. Serious baseball fans consider Nolan Ryan a superb major league pitcher.

2. According to statistics, the typical major league pitcher shows hitters his best stuff at age thirty.

3. But a recent baseball season was Ryan's twenty-fourth in the big leagues.

4. According to the radar guns, at this point in his long career, his fastballs sometimes reached speeds of one hundred miles per hour.

5. Ryan's amazing fastball made his curveball more effective.

1.2 A Closer Look at Subjects

Let's take a closer look at the subject of the clause. Simple subjects or key words within complete subjects are nouns, pronouns, or noun substitutes. The key word might be a single noun, a single pronoun, or a combination of the two.

Nouns

You might remember that a noun is the name of a person, place, thing, or idea. In this definition, the word *thing* means a concrete noun, something you can touch or experience through one of the senses, and the word *idea* means an abstract noun, something that you can't touch, something intangible.

These nouns are arranged in their respective groups:

Persons	Places	Things	Ideas
accountant	kitchen	butter	success
doctor	city	magazines	memories
mothers	Idaho	toothpaste	cheerfulness
Santa Claus	Disneyworld	Kleenex	Judaism

As you can see, nouns can be singular (one) or plural (more than one). Some are capitalized, and some are not.

1. The Noun-Marker Test

All of the listed nouns, except the capitalized ones, can follow the words *a, an,* or *the,* which are called *noun markers,* because they signal or "mark" the appearance of a noun. For instance, you can say *an accountant, the kitchen, the butter,* and *a success.* But you cannot get the same sense of completeness by saying *a beautiful* or *the scary,* because *beautiful* and *scary* are adjectives, not nouns.

2. The Subject Test for Nouns

Another way to see if a word is a noun is to try to use it as the subject of a sentence. If a word can be used in this way, it's either a noun or a pronoun.

Let's say, for instance, that we want to see if *decorate* and *decoration* are nouns. We can try each as the subject of a sentence:

(a) The *decorate* lit up the room.

(b) The *decoration* lit up the room.

This test quickly shows us that *decoration* is a noun but *decorate* is not. If you need to practice identifying nouns, try the next exercise.

Exercise 1.3

In each of the following pairs, one word is a noun and one is not. Use the noun-marker test or the subject test to decide which one is the noun. Then circle the noun in each pair.

1. begin, beginning
2. prediction, predict
3. organization, organize
4. liar, lied
5. gently, gentleness

6. decide, decision
7. allow, allowance
8. reliability, rely
9. collection, collect
10. defy, defiance

Most of the nouns in Exercise 1.3 are idea nouns; they're abstract. Notice how often they have the same word endings. Here are five common noun suffixes:-ance, -ity, -ment, -ness, and -tion.

Pronouns

Pronouns are words that take the place of nouns. We use them to avoid repeating a noun over and over. For example, instead of writing, "*Dancing* is a popular form of exercise. *Dancing* burns up two hundred to four hundred calories per hour," a student might want to change the subject of the second sentence to the pronoun *It,* which, in the context, would clearly mean dancing.

This chapter focuses on the pronoun's ability to function as a subject. But pronouns can do all sorts of other things in sentences, too. Let's look at three groups of pronouns that can be used as subjects of independent clauses. (Pronouns can be subjects of dependent clauses, too.)

12

Personal	Demonstrative	Indefinite
I	this	anybody
you	that	anyone
he	these	anything
she	those	everybody
it		everyone
we		everything
they		nobody
		no one
		nothing
		somebody
		someone
		something

It's not necessary to memorize these pronouns in their three groups, but it's essential to know that they are pronouns and can be the subjects of sentences.

Noun Substitutes

In addition to nouns and pronouns, other constructions can work as subjects. These are words, phrases, or clauses that perform the same job as a noun. (A *phrase* is any series of two or more words that is less than a clause. A phrase might have a subject-type word or a word from the verb category, but not both.)

Let's look at a few examples of the main types of noun substitutes. In each case, a phrase does the same job a one-word noun could do.

1. Infinitive Verb Phrases

An infinitive verb phrase is any verb preceded by the word *to*. Examples are *to walk, to sing, to dream.* Look at this sentence:

13

To decide is to take a risk.

Here, the verb phrase *to decide* works like a noun and acts as the subject of the sentence. You can make a rough equivalent of this sentence by using a conventional noun as the subject:

A *decision* is always a risk.

2. Gerund Phrases

A gerund is a verb that ends in *-ing* and works as a noun. A gerund phrase is simply a gerund plus other words attached to it. Here's an example:

Planning an overseas trip takes a tremendous effort.

You can see that the subject here is roughly equivalent to the noun subject in the sentence:

A *plan for an overseas trip* takes a tremendous effort to create.

3. Prepositional Phrases

Most prepositions are direction or relationship words such as *at, behind, inside,* and *toward.* A prepositional phrase is a preposition plus the noun or pronoun that follows it. Prepositional phrases can also work as subjects:

Before breakfast is a good time for a walk.

Under the boardwalk was the place to be.

4. Clauses

Infinitive verb phrases, gerund phrases, and prepositional phrases are common constructions that can do the job of a noun. Therefore, they can be subjects of clauses. (They can also be objects of verbs.) But these are not the only noun substitutes, just the most common ones. Other constructions can act

14

as nouns. For example, a whole *clause* can act as a subject within a larger clause:

What really gripes me is wilted brown lettuce in a high-priced salad.

Can you see how the subject in this sentence is similar to the noun phrase *My complaint* or *My pet peeve?*
You don't have to be too concerned about the names of these constructions. But it is important to remember:

1. what the job of the subject is (to present a topic for the predicate to make a statement about by showing the subject's action or condition), and

2. that nouns, pronouns, or a variety of other substitutes acting as nouns can do that job.

Exercise 1.4

Find the subject of each sentence. Draw a line under the subject and write s above it. (It will help to find the verb first.) All the subjects here are drawn from the noun substitute category.

1. To work hard today is to believe in tomorrow.

2. What the world needs now is love, sweet love.

3. Tracking students into so-called ability groups often creates great damage of both an intellectual and an emotional nature.

4. Outside that crazy office is where she wanted to be.

5. What a racist or sexist joke reveals about its teller is quite astonishing.

15

1.3 A Closer Look at Predicates

Now let's look more closely at the part of the sentence that makes a statement about the subject—the predicate.

Verbs

As noted earlier, verbs either show the action—whether visible or invisible—or the condition of a subject. Those that show the condition of the subject do so by linking the subject to a complement that follows the verb.

Another important fact is that verbs change in form to communicate changes in time. These various forms are called a verb's *tenses*. Sometimes forming a verb tense involves nothing more than the addition of an ending; for example, adding a *-d* or *-ed* ending can form the past tense of a regular verb. But other times it involves the addition of a *helping verb*, which is simply a verb that helps another verb form a particular tense or a mood. Helping verbs include forms of the verb *to be* such as *is, are, was, were,* and *will be*. They also include forms of the verb *to have,* such as *has, have,* and *had*.

Other helping verbs are the modal auxiliaries: *can, could, may, might, shall, should, must, will,* and *would*.

There are also helping verbs that give extra emphasis to the predicate: *do, does,* and *did*.

When a verb joins up with a helping verb, it forms a *verb phrase*. For example: *is living, will be reviewed, has answered, could remember, might sing,* and *did pay*. Other verb phrases contain more than one helper. Examples are: *will have been dedicated, should be invited,* and *may have promised*.

Changing Tenses: Regular Verbs versus Irregular Verbs

The past tense of regular verbs is formed by adding *-d* or *-ed*. For example, the present tense *I smile* becomes the past tense *I smiled. They want* becomes they *wanted*. Most verbs are regular verbs.

Irregular verbs do not follow the same pattern. To change the tense of an irregular verb, you do not add *-d* or *-ed*. The base form might not change at all, it might take a spelling change other than the addition of *-d* or *-ed,* or it might change only its pronunciation. See Chapter 6, pages 137-143, for more discussion on regular and irregular verbs and for a list of common irregular verbs.

Exercise 1.5

For the following sentences:

(a) Write *s* over the key word or words in the subject.

(b) Write *v* over the verb or verb phrase. (Create you own marking system to show that an element contains more than one word.)

(c) Label other structurally important elements in the predicate—if there are any—with *sub com, ob com, do,* and *io.*

1. According to a recent study, even mild sleep deprivation can prevent the retention of new and complex knowledge.

2. For centuries, the tongue, with its various colors, textures, and patterns, has given doctors a mirror of the condition of the rest of the body.

3. By November 1964, Malcolm X had made three trips to Africa and had altered his position on the possibility of black and white cooperation and harmony.

4. *Nintendo Power* magazine is published every other month.

5. In his later works, Vincent van Gogh painted his suns a brilliant yellow.

6. *Competition* has been defined as mutually exclusive goal attainment.

7. Perhaps Chester F. Carlson should have named his invention, the copying machine and forerunner of the Xerox machine, after himself.

8. Standard male mannequins wear size 40 regular.

9. Since the beginning of the last Ice Age, the size of human teeth has been decreasing at the rate of one percent every two thousand years.

10. According to experts in nutrition, most people with occasional mood swings should blame their diet, not their ancestry or sheer bad luck.

More About Completing Elements in the Predicate

You have already learned about the different kinds of completing elements that help a verb make a clearer or fuller statement about a subject. You learned that subject complements follow linking verbs; direct objects and indirect objects follow certain action verbs; and object complements follow some direct objects.

The completing elements you worked with earlier were simple—usually a single noun, pronoun, or adjective. Now we'll examine more unusual objects and complements. Three sources of unusual objects and complements are *infinitive verb phrases, prepositional phrases,* and *gerunds and gerund phrases.*

An infinitive verb phrase is any verb in its base form preceded by the word to. Infinitive verb phrases are used to complete verbs here:

(a) He loves to *fly.*

(b) She plans *to compete.*

(c) They want *to surrender.*

These examples show prepositional phrases used as completing elements:

(d) The students went *over the notes.*

(e) He is *without resources.*

(f) The child abuser was *beneath contempt.*

Here gerunds—nouns formed from verbs with *-ing* endings—and gerund phrases serve as completing elements in the predicate:

(g) We attempted *placing the bets.*

(h) I like *playing tennis.*

(i) The director requests loud *singing* on the next number.

1.4 The Modifiers

Up to this point, we have focused on the parts that form the kernal of the clause: the simple subject, the verb, and the completing elements such as complements and objects. These parts can be visualized in another, structural way: They form the skeleton of the clause.

Now we're going to turn our attention to the parts that *modify,* or *describe,* the kernel. These words can be thought of as decorations, because they elaborate on the essential parts of the clause. They add flesh to the skeleton. Sometimes, however, these modifiers are themselves part of the kernel, namely, when they serve as completing elements after verbs.

We'll discuss four types of modifers: *adjectives, adverbs, prepositional phrases,* and *appositives.*

Better Sentence-Writing

Adjectives

Adjectives, as you know, are words used to describe nouns and pronouns. In English, adjectives usually precede the words they describe. Here are some examples:

(a) This is an *aggressive* team.

(b) She has a *terrific* attitude.

(c) It is a *beautiful* sculpture.

But, as you know, adjectives also can follow the words they describe *if* they are used as complements. For example:

(d) This team is *aggressive*.

(e) Her attitude is *terrific*.

(f) The sculpture is *beautiful*.

Exercise 1.6

Circle the objectives in the sentences below.

1. She sat on the polished oak desk.
2. The biggest problem seemed small.
3. He feared a negative reaction to his best work.
4. I heard a deep, raspy voice.
5. The persistent inflation called for drastic measures.
6. Our supporting evidence was historical.
7. We fished in the crystal waters and hoped for big pike.

8. The tallest man in the group served old-fashioned blackberry pie to the ladies.

9. The final assignment was difficult and challenging.

10. I was struck by the dramatic contrast between her sunburnt arms and pale white face.

You might have noticed how certain words can be adjectives in one context and nouns in another. For example, in Exercise 1.6 the word *blackberry* is an adjective because it describes the pie. But what is the same word in this sentence: "I found only one moldy *blackberry* in the box"? That's right—it's a noun; here, we're talking about an actual blackberry, not something that is described as blackberry in flavor or type.

Adverbs

We usually think of adverbs as words that modify verbs and end in *-ly*. Many adverbs do. But they don't have to end in *-ly*, and they can describe other modifiers—both adjectives and other adverbs. Our focus here is on basic sentence structure, however, so we will discuss only how adverbs modify verbs.

Adverbs can appear almost anywhere in a sentence. In the following sentences, the adverb is italicized, and the verb that the adverb modifies or describes is marked with a *v*:

$$v$$

(a) The children sucked their thumbs *loudly.*

$$v$$

(b) I tiptoed *quietly* into the corridor.

$$v$$

(c) *Eventually* we learned the truth.

$$v$$

(d) The doctors *later* spoke to the press.

$$v$$

(e) She spends too much time *there.*

21

Better Sentence-Writing

Some adverbs tell how an action is done: *How* did the children suck their thumbs? *Loudly. How* did I tiptoe into the corridor? *Quietly.*
Another group of adverbs tell *when* an action happens: *When* did we learn the truth? *Eventually.* When did the doctors speak to the press? *Later.*
A third group of adverbs tell *where* an action happens: *Where* does she spend too much time? *There. Where* did the secretary deliver the package? *Here.*
Adverbs don't have a great bearing on sentence structure. However, it is important to realize that adverbs sometimes appear in the *middle* of verb phrases. For example:

Northern Exposure is praised for its quirky, humane portrayal of life in Cicely, Alaska.

Appositives

Appositives are another kind of modifier. They are noun phrases that follow and describe other nouns. Although they can appear after any noun, in this chapter we'll look at how they often follow the simple subject of a clause. Here are some appositives that describe various U.S. presidents:

(a) Calvin Coolidge, *the thirtieth president,* walked a pet raccoon on a leash.

(b) Jimmy Carter, *a former peanut farmer,* was undone by the hostage crisis in Iran.

(c) Andrew Johnson, *a skilled tailor,* made most of his own clothes.

(d) Ronald Reagan, *a former actor,* took the role of president in 1980.

You can see how each appositive is a noun phrase that follows and describes another noun. You also can see that when appositives are used in this position—between the simple subject and the predicate of a clause—they are set off by commas.

Exercise 1.7

The following simple sentences, like the example sentences, contain bits of information about U.S. presidents, and each one has an appositive. For each sentence:

(a) Label the structurally important parts of each clause: the simple subjects *(s)*, verbs *(v)*, complements *(ob com* or *sub com* and direct objects *do)*.

(b) Draw a wavy line under the appositive in each sentence and set it off with beginning and ending commas.

(c) Write the kernel of each clause on the line provided. Remember that the kernel omits all the modifiers and contains only the structural essentials of the clause.

1. George Washington the first president of the United States loved peanut soup.

   Kernel: _____

2. John Quincy Adams the sixth president liked swimming in the nude in the Potomac River every morning at five o'clock.

   Kernel: _____

3. Zachary Taylor a career officer in the army for most of his life voted for the first time at the age of 62.

   Kernel: _____

4. James Buchanan president from 1857 to 1861 was a bachelor throughout his entire life.

   Kernel: _____

23

5. Abraham Lincoln an extremely persistent individual won the presidency in 1860 after eight election losses in a row.

Kernel: _____

Note: Adjective and adverb phrases also can follow and modify the subject of a clause. Like appositives, these phrases are set off by commas when they appear between the subject and verb of a clause. For example, in this sentence an adjective phrase describes the subject:

The child, *intelligent and strong*, took after her parents.

Here, an adverb phrase is the modifier:

The woman, *cautiously at first*, planted the seeds under a thin layer of reddish dirt.

Prepositional Phrases

Prepositional phrases are probably the most difficult modifiers to learn because there are so many of them. Before we define these phrases, let's look at an example. Underline the modifiers in this phrase:

the high cost of textbooks

The word *high* is obviously a modifier—an adjective, to be precise. But the words *of textbooks* make up another type of modifier—a prepositional phrase. The words *of textbooks* describe the noun *cost* just as surely as the adjective *high* does. We are talking about a high cost, not a low cost. Similarly, we are talking about the cost of textbooks, not the cost of banana splits. So *of textbooks* is a prepositional phrase that works as an adjective.

Here's an example of a prepositional phrase that acts as an adverb:

The boy dialed 911 in a panic.

How did he dial the number? He dialed it *in a panic*, not in a cool, calm frame of mind. In other words, *in a panic* modifies the verb *dialed*.
Prepositional phrases also can describe where an action was done. For example:

The man wrote his novel *at a seaside hotel*.

Or they can describe *when* an action was done. For example:

My mother graduated from law school *in May*.

Most prepositions can be thought of as *direction* or *relationship* words. The noun or pronoun that follows a preposition is called the object of the preposition. Taken together, the preposition and its object form a prepositional phrase. An important thing to know when editing your work is that the subject of a sentence will never be inside a prepositional phrase. Knowing this fact will help to solve problems of subject-verb agreement, a topic we will review later in this book.
Here is a list of common prepositions, each used in the context of a prepositional phrase. The words in italics are the prepositions.

about the introduction	*above* his head
across the border	*after* recess
against his principles	*along* those lines
among ourselves	*around* our city
at the time	*before* the meeting

behind her	*below* the ice
beneath the top layer	*beside* her mother
between two slices	*beyond* tomorrow
by them	*despite* my wishes
down the path	*during* the first minute
except you	*for* my children
from his grandmother	*in* the spirit
inside his mind	*into* the grocery store
like a winner	*near* her heart
of the joke	*off* the top
on the dresser	*onto* the floor
out the door	*outside* the solar system
over the noodles	*past* his house
since her graduation	*through* the middle
throughout the poem	*to* my office
toward the future	*under* it
underneath the books	*until* winter
up the steps	*upon* her entrance
with love	*within* your lifetime
without regrets	

There are also *phrasal prepositions.* These are prepositions that are made up of two or more words. Here are a few examples, again given in the context of a prepositional phrase. The phrasal prepositions are in italics:

according to Mark	*along with* fried clams
because of my sister	*except for* him

in addition to the readings	*in case of* emergency
in place of the party	*in spite of* your absence
instead of television	*out of* luck
up to par	*with reference to* the letter
with regard to your request	

Exercise 1.8

Use the labels *s, v, sub com, ob com, do* and *io* to mark the key parts of the following simple sentences. Draw a wavy line under appositives and cross out prepositional phrases and other modifiers. Then write the kernel on the line provided.

1. Robin Burns, the highest-paid woman in the United States, is the chief executive officer of Estée Lauder USA.

   Kernel: _____

2. During the early part of his career, Babe Ruth pitched.

   Kernel: _____

3. In 1981, the number of foreign tourists in the United States exceeded the number of American tourists in foreign countries for the first time in the memory of record keepers in the travel industry.

   Kernel: _____

4. For some strange reason, the color of raspberry popsicles has always been blue.

   Kernel: _____

Better Sentence-Writing

5. The Treasury Department of the United States dry-cleaned soiled money during the administration of President Woodrow Wilson.

   Kernel: _____

6. According to experts in animal behavior, a female tree frog instinctively recognizes the connection between the volume of a male tree frog's song and his physical strength and vigor, prime factors in his desirability as a mate.

   Kernel: _____

7. The headquarters of the McDonald's Corporation in Illinois has a 700-gallon burger-shaped waterbed.

   Kernel: _____

8. The decaying organic matter on the floor of a forest is duff.

   Kernel: _____

9. The average size of the winner of the male division of the Boston Marathon over the years is 5 feet and 7 inches and 135 pounds.

   Kernel: _____

10. Ironically, country singer Hank Williams's last record before his death in 1953 at the young age of 29 was "I'll Never Get Out of this World Alive."

    Kernel: _____

Chapter 2

Sentence Combining: Basic Strategies and Common Problems

2.1 Compound Sentences

One of the easiest ways to combine clauses is to link them with a conjunction. The easiest conjunctions to work with are the *coordinating conjunctions*. Traditionally, seven words are listed in this category:

and	or
but	so
for	yet
nor	

Here are some examples of *compound sentences:*

1. Ernest Lawrence Thayer wrote "Casey at the Bat," **and** the San Francisco *Examiner* first published it on June 3, 1888.

2. Toni Morrison is probably America's finest working novelist, **but** she is also a first-rate essayist and editor.

3. According to M. Scott Peck, M.D., in *People of the Lie*, evil people attack others, **yet** they rarely face their own failures as human beings.

Label the subjects, verbs, complements, and objects in the preceding sentences so that you see clearly how each sentence is made up of two clauses. The clauses are *independent,* which means that they can stand on their own. Each one could be written as a simple sentence, which is one independent clause. In a compound sentence, two independent clauses are joined with one of the coordinating conjunctions.

Notice also that a *comma* is used in a compound sentence. It is placed after the first clause, just before the conjunction.

This does not mean that a comma is always used before *and, but, for, nor, or, so*, and *yet*. For example, look at these sentences:

(a) Orange **and** green are two of the secondary colors.

(b) New college graduates are often excited **but** apprehensive about the next phase of their lives.

No comma is used in either sentence because in these cases *and* and *but* are not used to connect clauses.

Exercise 2.1

All of the sentences below are compound sentences. Label both clauses of each sentence, using *s, v, do, io, sub com,* and *ob com.* Circle the conjunction that connects the clauses; then insert a comma before the conjunction.

1. On the average, Mexican-Americans have larger families than any other ethnic group in the United States and they can also claim the lowest divorce rate of all.

2. In the fifteenth century, French gardeners wanted the sweetest possible melons so they watered them with sugar water and honey.

3. Facial tissues are great for cold sufferers but those thin little sheets were actually invented for the removal of cold cream.

4. Both Bill Wilson, a New York stockbroker, and Robert H. Smith, an Ohio surgeon, had a drinking problem so they joined forces and started Alcoholics Anonymous in 1935.

5. Most people keep their New Year's resolutions for no more than a few weeks or they don't make them in the first place.

Important Note: As you've learned, the coordinating conjunctions are usually used to connect two independent clauses, but they can also be used to connect more than two clauses within one sentence. Analyze and punctuate the following example. Circle the conjunctions that connect the clauses and insert a comma before each:

At the age of 23, Frank Church of Idaho learned of his incurable cancer but he lived another 36 years and in that time he became one of the century's most powerful and effective U.S. senators

You can see that *three* independent clauses have been connected by coordinating conjunctions in the sentence about Senator Frank Church. This is a useful option for combining clauses, but, of course, you should not overuse it because you know that variety in sentence structure is a mark of good, lively writing. Three or four clauses combined with coordinating conjunctions would probably be the limit within one sentence. Keep in mind that the standard and most common use of the coordinating conjunction is simply to bring together two clauses.

••

2.2 Complex Sentences
••

Complex sentences are another easy technique of sentence combination, and they provide even more variety in your writing because most of them can be presented in two different sequences. In a complex sentence, the conjunction can be placed between the clauses, just as in a compound sentence. For example:

(a) The mandrill of Western Africa is often called the most colorful mammal in the world **because** it has a brilliant crimson nose and bright blue cheeks.

Or the conjunction (the word because) can be placed before the first clause in a complex sentence. For example:

(b) **Because** it has a brilliant crimson nose and bright blue cheeks, the mandrill of western Africa is often called the most colorful mammal in the world.

In both the (a) and (b) sentences, the clause that comes right after the conjunction is called the *dependent clause*. It's called dependent because it depends upon more information. It can't stand alone. *Because it has a brilliant crimson nose and bright blue cheeks* doesn't make sense by itself. It needs something else, namely an independent clause. Once it is attached to an independent clause, such as *the mandrill of western Africa is often called the most colorful mammal in the world*, the two clauses work together to make a perfectly good sentence—a *complex* sentence.

A Note on Punctuation

If you're especially observant, you may already have noticed that a comma is used in the preceding examples only when the conjunction appears at the start of the first clause; then a comma is placed between the dependent clause and the independent clause. A comma is not generally used in a complex sentence when the conjunction appears before the second clause; in other words, you don't use a comma when the conjunction is in the middle of a complex sentence. Here is another way to say this:

dependent clause first → comma between clauses

independent clause first → no comma

There are exceptions to this rule, and later you might want to learn about them and about some other fine points, but in this book, we are concerned with the basics, and this punctuation rule is correct for the vast majority of complex sentences that you will write.

Subordinating Conjunctions

So far, we've looked at just one of the *subordinating conjunctions*, that are used to make complex sentences, but there are others. These are the most commonly used:

after	because	that	whenever
although	before	though	where
as	if	unless	wherever
as long as	since	until	while
as soon as	so that	when	why

You need to be able to recognize both coordinating and subordinating conjunctions when you see them in sentences.

Better Sentence-Writing

Exercise 2.2

Label the two clauses in each complex sentence. Circle the conjunction that connects the clauses. Then follow the punctuation rules for complex sentences.

1. When you lick a postage stamp you consume one-tenth of one calorie.

2. The birth of the Dionne quintuplets in 1934 created an enormous sensation because no other set of identical quintuplets had ever survived.

3. Although Pretty Boy Floyd was originally known for his string of bank robberies he gained even greater fame for his uncanny knack of avoiding police traps.

4. Eight thousand people must live in a community before the U.S. government calls it a city.

5. If F. Scott Fitzgerald had completed *The Last Tycoon* before his death in 1940 at the age of 44 it might have been a major American novel.

A Final Note

You may have noticed that some of the subordinating conjunctions were listed earlier as prepositions. Don't let this confuse you. Some words can be used as both subordinating conjunctions and prepositions, depending on how they are used.

1. (a) Wendy went to the Halloween party *after* school.
   (b) She had to go back for her broom *after* she left the party.

2. (a) I'd like to see you *before* the spring break starts on Monday.
   (b) I'd like to see you *before* the spring break.

3. (a) Daniel wasn't completely at home in Detroit *until* his third year there.
   (b) *Until* Daniel had been in Detroit for three years, he wasn't completely at home in the city.

* *

2.3 Embedded Sentences
* *

Another very valuable strategy for combining sentences is *embedding*. At first this might seem less familiar to you than the process by which you form compound and complex sentences. But if you look at a large sampling of your own writing, you're sure to find examples of embedded sentences. You are already creating them, so it's just a matter of becoming more conscious of how the process works and learning the fine points of punctuation.

This process does not involve conjunctions. It involves *relative pronouns*, and these are the most important ones:

who

whose

which

(The word *that* can also be used for embedding, but we'll deal with it in Chapter 3 because it involves a different punctuation rule.)

Let's say that you wanted to combine these two sentences:

(a) Eudora Welty is a major Southern writer.

(b) She was born in Mississippi in 1909.

If you try to combine clauses (a) and (b) to make a compound or a complex sentence, you'll find that none of the conjunctions seems quite right. Sure, you could probably say, "Eudora Welty is a major Southern writer, and she was born in Mississippi in 1909," but doesn't that sentence have a weak, flat sound to it?

Better Sentence-Writing

The process of embedding, on the other hand, works well with clauses (a) and (b). The first thing we have to do is change the subject of the second clause to a relative pronoun. Here's what we do:

who
(b) She was born in Mississippi in 1909.

Then we insert the new clause (b) between the subject and predicate of the (a) clause. Now this is what we have:

Eudora Welty **who was born in Mississippi in 1909** is a major Southern writer.

As a finishing touch, we'll add two commas—one before and one after the clause we have embedded. And here's our final product, an embedded sentence:

Eudora Welty, who was born in Mississippi in 1909, is a major Southern writer.

The commas set the *embedded clause* off from the *main clause*, making the whole sentence much easier to read.

Exercise 2.3

Combine these sets of sentences by using the embedding process. Remember to insert commas around the embedded clause. (Again, the relative pronouns we are using are *which, who,* and *whose.*)

1. (a) Thomas Jefferson was broke when he died.
   (b) He was certainly one of America's most brilliant presidents.

_____

_____

_____

2. (a) Monrovia was founded in 1822 and named after President James Monroe.
   (b) It is the capital of the West African nation of Liberia.

   _____

   _____

   _____

3. (a) Herbert Hoover was supposedly worried that King Tut was becoming too attached to other people.
   (b) He once gave an order that no White House staffers were to pet his dog.

   _____

   _____

   _____

4. (a) James Buchanan was the only president to remain a bachelor.
   (b) His 23-year-old fiancé broke off their engagement and died mysteriously a short time later.

   _____

   _____

   _____

5. (a) Grover Cleveland's duties as a sheriff in New York State resulted in his participation in the execution of two convicted murderers.
   (b) They included serving as one county's official hangman.

   _____

   _____

   _____

Better Sentence-Writing

Two Variations of Embedded Sentences

Some of the embedded sentences that are made with the words who and which can be reworked in two ways. Knowing how to create these two variations will give you a little more flexibility in your writing.

Look at this example. First, we will combine two sentences by embedding, just as you did in the last exercise. We'll use these two simple sentences:

(a) Flashlight fish blink their lights to attract their prey.

(b) They are equipped with glowing pockets of bacteria beneath each eye.

When they are combined by embedding, we have:

1. Flashlight fish, which are equipped with glowing pockets of bacteria beneath each eye, blink their lights to attract their prey.

Sentence 1 is the type of sentence you were creating in the last exercise, but we're going to start calling it a "full embedding" or a "fully embedded" sentence.

Now we're going to make the first variation. We simply drop the relative pronoun *(which)* and the helping or linking verb *(are)*. With what we have left, we make a "reduced embedding":

2. Flashlight fish, *equipped with glowing pockets of bacteria beneath each eye*, blink their lights to attract their prey.

Now we're going to try the other variation. All we do is take the words that appear between the commas in sentence 2 and use them as an introductory phrase. Now we have:

3. **Equipped with glowing pockets of bacteria beneath each eye**, flashlight fish blink their lights to attract their prey.

38

2.3 Embedded Sentences

Sentence 3 is the "moved embedding." Notice that we haven't changed any wording when we went from 2 to 3. All we did was change the order of the words. Also notice that the reduced embedding takes two commas. The moved variation takes only one.

Exercise 2.4

Here are five fully embedded sentences. Practice working out the two variations for each.

1. A quetzal, which is unable to take off into the air like other birds, has to jump off a tree branch backward to avoid snagging its 24-inch tail.

   Reduced: _____

   _____

   _____

   Moved: _____

   _____

   _____

2. Male narwhals, which are nicknamed "unicorns of the sea," sport a single nine-foot-long tusk.

   Reduced: _____

   _____

   _____

   Moved: _____

   _____

   _____

3. Some biologists, who are puzzled by the hump on the back of the thorny devil, speculate that the lizard can push the hump up to create the illusion of a second head when it wants to confuse its enemies.

Reduced: _____

_____

_____

Moved: _____

_____

_____

4. A sloth, which is blessed with three very efficient curved claws on each foot, normally hangs from a tree for its daily 18-hour snooze.

Reduced: _____

_____

_____

Moved: _____

_____

_____

5. One scientist, who was curious about the basic color of the zebra, conducted a study and concluded that zebras are actually black with white stripes, not white with black stripes.

Reduced: _____

_____

_____

Moved: _____

_____

_____

• •
2.4 A Sentence-Combining Approach to the Problem of Run-ons and Comma Splices
• •

Up to this point, you have been working with various methods of combining sentences. Now we're going to turn our attention to two different types of errors that can easily occur during the process of sentence combining.

The first is the problem of *run-ons*. If run-ons have always been a problem in your writing, now you have some good sentence-combining techniques to use in solving them. In later chapters, you'll learn even more techniques.

What exactly is a run-on? It's actually a very simple sentence structure error. A run-on is a series of two or more unconnected independent clauses. Here is an example:

The Daughters of St. Crispin was founded in 1869 in Lynn,

Massachusetts it was the first national organization of trade

union women.

Label the key structural components example so that you can clearly see the two clauses. Then write *RO* where one sentence "runs on" into the other.

When teachers see this kind of sentence in a student's writing, they know that the student is attempting to combine clauses. They know it from the placement of the two clauses between one capital letter and period. But the two clauses are *not* combined or connected. Instead, they are running into one another.

41

Better Sentence-Writing

How can you solve the run-on? A comma after the word *Massachusetts* cannot join the clauses. That "solution" would simply create another error—a comma splice. You *can* solve the run-on in a number of ways, using the techniques you've learned in this chapter. The following are four solutions. Notice that the solutions are compound, complex, and embedded sentences. In other words, the solutions are types of sentence combinations you have been studying in the preceding units. Here are the four possible solutions for the run-on:

(a) The Daughters of St. Crispin, which was the first national organization of trade union women, was rounded in 1869 in Lynn, Massachusetts.

(b) The Daughters of St. Crispin was rounded in 1869 in Lynn, Massachusetts, and it was the first national organization of trade union women.

(c) When the Daughters of St. Crispin was founded in 1869 in Lynn, Massachusetts, it was the first national organization of trade union women.

(d) Founded in 1869 in Lynn, Massachusetts, the Daughters of St. Crispin was the first national organization of trade union women.

As you can see, (a) is a fully embedded sentence, (b) is compound, (c) is complex, and (d) is a variation of an embedded and reduced sentence that was produced after juggling the parts of the sentence a bit. These are all good techniques for solving run-ons, and you'll learn more strategies later.

Combining, Not Breaking Up

Notice that we did not solve the run-on about the Daughters of St. Crispin by breaking apart the two clauses and making two separate sentences, each with its own capital letter and period. Breaking run-ons up into separate sentences is a good technique to use in the early grades, but for adult writers, it is

42

usually inappropriate. You *should* be combining clauses, but you have to do it correctly. Use a period and a capital letter when your run-on or comma splice is long enough that it might be difficult for your reader to follow your writing, or when you want to write a short, perhaps choppy sentence for a strong, simple, or dramatic effect. But for most students, those two cases are the exception. In the great majority of cases, run-ons and comma splices should be corrected by combining clauses, not by separating them.

Three Things to Realize About Run-ons and Comma Splices

There are three important things to remember about run-ons. First of all, they aren't necessarily long. These are all run-ons:

(a) He walked she ran.

(b) The vegetables were fresh they were great.

(c) Dogs bark cats meow.

(d) Nancy loved antiques, she disliked most modern things.

(e) The picnic was postponed, it rained.

(f) The first semester was hard, the second one was a little better.

Notice that the first three examples do not contain a comma between the clauses, and the last three examples do. Examples (d) through (f) are technically called *comma splices*, but they are a sentence structure error so similar to run-ons that both types of mistakes are frequently just called *run-ons* to keep things simple. Try to solve each of the six errors above, using the sentence-combining techniques that you know.

The second important fact about run-ons and comma splices is that the second clause often begins with a pronoun. Go back and see how many examples in our discussion show this pattern. If you watch for this tendency in your own writing, you'll prevent a lot of problems. Let's suppose you wrote,

"Christopher wants to eat, he is starved." When you wrote "he is starved," you produced an independent clause, which must be connected to the clause before it. The fact that *he* refers to *Christopher* in the first clause does not mean that the two clauses are already connected.

Here's the third point. The word *that* can attach one clause to another clause as a complement. So the following examples are *not* run-ons. They are perfectly acceptable sentences because the word *that* makes the second clause the complement of the first clause. The clauses are connected by the word *that*.

(a) Charlene knew that Mike was right.

(b) The managers of both stores thought that they could solve their problems alone.

(c) Mary Ann and Bobby hoped that their baby would be on time.

Exercise 2.5

Label each sentence *OK, CS,* or *RO*. Mark the spot where one sentence runs on or splices into the other. Then rewrite the problem sentences, using sentence-combining techniques where possible. Please use your own paper for the rewrites for this exercise and all the other exercises in this unit.

1. _____ Diamonds have a certain mystique about them this has been true for over 2,700 years.

2. _____ The first diamonds were discovered along riverbeds in south central India, they were found about 800 B.C.

3. _____ South central India was the primary source of diamonds for about two thousand years, then South America became the major source, later South Africa did.

4. _____ Although South Africa is the location of the best diamond mines in the world, diamonds are also found in many other places, including other parts of Africa, Australia, Russia, and the United States.

5. _____ In the United States, there are 19 diamond mines, most are around the border between Colorado and Wyoming.

Exercise 2.6

Label each sentence OK, CS, or RO. Mark the spot where one sentence runs on or splices into the other. Then rewrite problem sentences, using sentence-combining techniques where possible.

1. _____ How do you know a good diamond when you see one?

2. _____ Diamonds are judged on the basis of the three Cs, the three Cs are carats, cut, and clarity.

3. _____ The word *carat* comes from the Greek word *keration,* which means "carob seed" carob seeds were used to measure the weight of diamonds long ago in India.

4. _____ In the modern world of diamond dealing, a carat is a more standard measure it represents $\frac{1}{142}$ of an ounce.

5. _____ The largest diamond ever found was 3,106 carats, that equals about 1.3 pounds.

• •
2.5 A Sentence-Combining Approach to the Problem of Fragments
• •

Another problem that can be solved by sentence combining is that of *fragments*. In the last unit, you learned that run-ons and comma splices are not always long, and in this unit, you'll learn that fragments are not always short.

What is a fragment? As you might expect from the name, it is a *piece* or a *part* of something. A fragment is only part of a sentence, but it's "pretending" to be a whole sentence. In what way does it pretend to be a sentence? It does this by starting out with a capital letter and ending with a period. A fragment is a group of words that is set up between a capital letter and a period even though it does not meet all three of the requirements of a sentence. To be a sentence, a group of words must have three things:

1. a subject

2. a predicate

3. a sense of independence

In other words, a fragment might have one or two of these ingredients, but it doesn't have all three. If it did, it would be a sentence, not just part of one.

The problem of fragments is not one that all students have. In fact, many more students have a problem with run-ons and comma splices. But when adult writers do have a hard time with fragments, their fragments usually take a number of different forms, and that fact, of course, makes working with fragments a bit of a challenge. We're going to take a look at the four types of fragments that appear most often in the work of college students.

Type 1: Dependent Clause Set Up as a Sentence

A type 1 fragment is the simplest type of fragment, and it should be especially easy to spot now that you've worked with complex sentences. This fragment has a subject and a predicate, but it does not have a sense of independence. It lacks that because a conjunction has been attached to it. When we say that it lacks a sense of independence, we mean that it can't stand on its own as a unit of communication. The conjunction makes the reader expect to be told more than the information in the dependent clause. Here are some examples of dependent clause fragments:

(a) **Because** goldfish were supposed to bring love and harmony to an Egyptian household in ancient times.

(b) **If** the color red really does scare witches away.

(c) **Although** the word *bride* comes from an Old English word for "cook."

Items (a), (b), and (c) are perfectly good clauses, but they are not whole sentences. That's why they cannot be set up between a capital letter and a period. Once you add a subordinating conjunction to the beginning of a clause, that clause has been "marked" for combination with another clause. Then you have two choices: You can combine the dependent clause with an independent one, which will give the sentence its sense of independence, or you can remove the conjunction and make the clause a simple sentence. Here are possible revisions:

(a) Goldfish were supposed to bring love and harmony to an Egyptian household in ancient times.

(b) The color red really does scare witches away.

(c) Not all newlywed brides are talented in the kitchen, although the word *bride* comes from an Old English word for "cook."

47

Special note: Whenever you start a sentence with one of the subordinating conjunctions, you can be sure that if the sentence has only one clause, you've got a fragment. But you do not always have a fragment if you start a simple sentence with one of the coordinating conjunctions. Sometimes those seven—*and, but, for, nor, or, so,* and *yet*—are used as transitions at the beginning of a simple sentence.

For instance, there's no fragment here: "I told him never to come here again. *And* I meant it." *And I meant it* has been written as a separate sentence to give it strong emphasis, and that's fine. If the writer did not want the emphasis that comes from a new sentence, he or she could have written, "I told him never to come here again, *and* I meant it." Either way is acceptable.

Type 2: Fragment Involving an *-ing* Verb

A type 2 fragment may look less familiar, but it's not difficult to understand. This type also has a subject and a predicate and lacks a sense of independence. But this time there is no conjunction involved. Here the problem is an *-ing* verb used alone in a sentence of one clause. For example:

1. Many African-Americans joyfully **celebrating** Kwanzaa each winter.

2. The tradition of Easter eggs **having** its roots in early Germanic custom.

3. The pearl **being** an essential ingredient in many love potions.

Each of these three fragments has a subject and a predicate, but the *-ing* verb used alone robs each one of its sense of independence.

To solve this type of fragment, you can use three different approaches. One is to add a helping verb. For example:

1. (a) Many African-Americans **are** joyfully **celebrating** Kwanzaa each winter.

We added the helping verb *are.*
Another method is to change the *-ing* verb to a different verb form. For example:

2. (a) The tradition of Easter eggs **had** its roots in early Germanic custom.

We changed *having* to *had.*
A third solution calls for treating the *-ing* verb and the words after it as a phrase that describes the subject. Then you add an entirely new predicate to the sentence. For example:

3. (a) The pearl, being an essential ingredient in many love potions, **was highly valued by superstitious romantics.**

We added the predicate *was highly valued by superstitious romantics.*
A note about being: The word *being* is often the culprit in this type of fragment. *Being* is a form of the verb *to be.* So *being* should be changed to another form of the verb *to be*—a word such as *is, am, are, were,* or *will be.*

Type 3: Fragment Related to Embedding

Another type of fragment comes from a slipup in the embedding process. Here are three examples:

(a) The superstition **that** amethysts prevented drunkenness. Was widely believed by people in ancient times.

(b) A person **who** spills pepper. Is probably going to get into an argument with a good friend.

(c) Tattoos, **which** some sailors considered protection against drowning. At one time were also thought to prevent smallpox.

49

Better Sentence-Writing

After all the work you've done with embedding, the problem with these fragments should be clear. Each lettered item really contains two fragments. Each contains a subject that is set up as a full sentence and a predicate that is set up as a full sentence. To correct them, all you have to do is change capitalization and punctuation.

Another kind of fragment is a variation of this type. It begins with a relative pronoun, and it describes a noun or pronoun at the end of the sentence before it. For example:

The pepper was spilled by Pat. **Who any minute might find himself in an argument with his best friend John.**

To solve the fragment, change the period to a comma and make the capital *W* on *Who* lowercase.

Another way to avoid fragments that involve relative pronouns is simply to keep this rule in mind: *The only sentences that can begin with relative pronouns are questions.* These, for example, are perfectly fine. They're not fragments:

Who wrote *Jitterbug Perfume?*

Whose size 13 shoes are these?

Which pasta recipe works best?

Type 4: Cutoff Modifier

The last type of fragment involves a modifying phrase that is cut off from the sentence it describes. Here are some examples:

(a) **Used to cure headaches and insomnia.** Opium was extracted from poppies in Persia and Asia Minor for centuries before it was discovered in other parts of the world.

(b) **Hoping to keep a friendship from breaking up**. Some people whisper "bread and butter" whenever anything, such as another person, a tree, or a child on a bike, momentarily separates two friends out for a stroll.

(c) The ancient Greeks valued thyme highly. **Believing that the herb's fragrance restored one's energy**.

Again, you can see how easily these would be solved. Once more, it is just a matter of changing the period to a comma and making the following letter lowercase.

Exercise 2.7

Label each item *OK* or *F*. Then rewrite the fragments, using a variety of sentence-combining techniques. Please do the rewrites on your own paper.

1. _____ *The Statistical Abstract*, which is produced annually by the U.S. Commerce Department. Fills almost 1,000 pages.

2. _____ In one recent year, *The Statistical Abstract* offered a number of interesting tidbits of information about the 50 states in the union.

3. _____ Massachusetts, for example, being the state with the highest number of doctors per 100,000 people.

4. _____ The fact that New York has more lawyers per person than any other state.

5. _____ The state with the highest percentage of people over the age of 65 is, not surprisingly, Florida.

Better Sentence-Writing

Exercise 2.8

Label each item *OK* or *F.* Then rewrite the fragments, using a variety of techniques.

1. _____ *Cross Your Fingers, Spit in Your Hat*, which is a book about superstitions and folklore.

2. _____ The most interesting superstitions being the ones about love and marriage.

3. _____ Here are two especially quirky ones.

4. _____ If you pull a hair from the head of someone you love, he or she will love you back and love you deeply.

5. _____ The object of your desire will also love you if you give him or her a bowl of soup. Which is flavored with three drops of your blood.

Chapter 3

Punctuating Sentence Combinations

3.1 Using Commas in Compound and Complex Sentences (A Review)

As you know, one use of the comma is to punctuate compound and complex sentences. In the last chapter, you worked with compound and complex sentences, but there we were primarily interested in the structure of those sentence forms. Here our emphasis is on the punctuation of compound and complex sentences.

Compound Sentences

Here again are the coordinating conjunctions:

and	nor	so
but	or	yet
for		

The basic rule is this: *In a compound sentence, you insert a comma before the conjunction that joins two clauses.* Your writing teacher might tell you that sometimes it's okay to omit the comma if the clauses in a compound sentence are short and if there's no chance of confusion. That's true. But for the purpose of simplicity and for reinforcement of your knowledge of the basic rule, you should *insert a comma in all compound sentences in this chapter.* This is also the simplest rule to remember and use in your own writing.

Also remember that you don't put a comma before every *and* or *but* you see in a sentence. Make sure there's actually a clause both before and after the conjunction.

Complex Sentences

By now you know that these are the most important subordinating conjunctions.

after	because	that	whenever
although	before	though	where
as	if	unless	wherever
as long as	since	until	while
as soon as	so that	when	why

Remember that a subordinating conjunction can join clauses in two different ways: The conjunction can be placed before the first clause or before the second clause. When the conjunction is placed before the first clause, you use a comma between the clauses. When the conjunction is placed before the second clause, you normally don't use a comma between the clauses. Another way to say this is:

dependent clause first → comma between clauses

independent clause first → no comma

Here's a review exercise on recognizing and punctuating compound and complex sentences.

Exercise 3.1

Some of these sentences are compound, and others are complex. Please do the following: (1) Label each sentence *compound* or *complex*. (2) Circle the conjunction that joins the two clauses in each sentence. (3) Insert a comma if it is needed because a sentence is compound or because a sentence is complex with the dependent clause first. (Label subjects, verbs, complements, and objects if that helps you to see the two clauses in each sentence.)

1. _____ When it introduced box lunches on a flight to Paris in 1919 Handley Page Transport of England became the first airline to serve meals in flight.

2. _____ No one was surprised when Wilma P. Mankiller became the principal chief of the 72,000-member Cherokee nation.

3. _____ Most beer drinkers now buy their beer in cans but for 35 years bottled beer outsold canned beer.

4. _____ England's Queen Victoria wore mostly black for the remaining 39 years of her life after she lost her beloved husband Albert.

5. _____ Since Kahlil Gibran, the author of *The Prophet* and many other works, died in 1931 at the age of 48 the royalties from all posthumous sales have helped to the people of his impoverished native village of Bsharri in Lebanon.

Compound/Complex Sentences

Before we move on to other punctuation rules, we want to point out that some sentences are both compound and complex. They're called, not surprisingly, *compound/complex sentences*. You'll see that in such a sentence a writer uses a coordinating conjunction and a subordinating conjunction. Here are two examples.

(a) Because Jesus Christ died on the cross, many Christians assume that the symbol originated with Christ's death, but actually the cross had been used as a religious emblem for centuries before the crucifixion.

(b) This was the favorite saying of the great American actor Spencer Tracy: "You only live once, and if you work it right, once is enough."

3.2 Using Commas in Embedded Sentences

Like the unit you have just completed, this unit is partly a review of what you already know from your work in Chapter 2, but it also introduces a new idea.

Earlier we were interested primarily in how to make embedded sentences. Now let's look at how to punctuate them.

Example (a) is typical of the kind of embedded sentence you've already been dealing with. Please punctuate it.

(a) Pierre-Auguste Renoir who was born in 1841 never wanted to be known as a painter of modern life.

If you set off *who was born in 1841* with two commas, you're correct. This is the classic embedded sentence. In sentences like example (a) you have a clear subject—*Pierre-Auguste Renoir*— that is easily understood by the reader without the embedded information. In other words, *who was born in 1841* is extra information. It's interesting perhaps, but you don't need it in order to know what the subject of the sentence is; it's clear that the subject is *Pierre-Auguste Renoir*. When you have embedded information that is extra, meaning that you don't need it in order to identify the subject of the sentence, then you always set off that extra embedded information with two commas.

But there's another kind of sentence in which the embedded information is necessary to identify the subject. Look at this example and draw a wavy line under the embedded clause:

(b) All men who are irrationally and excessively submissive to their wives can be described as uxorious.

If you want to figure out if the embedded information is merely extra and not needed to identify the subject of the sentence, just omit it for a moment. Then you'll have: *All men can be described as uxorious.* That's not true, is it? If this rather odd and interesting word *uxorious* means "irrationally and excessively submissive to one's wife," then certainly you can't describe "all men" as uxorious.

In other words, the subject in (b) is not simply *All men.* The subject is really *All men who are irrationally and excessively submissive to their wives.* It's a particular kind of man the writer is talking about. The embedded words are not extra information added as an interesting aside after the subject. The embedded clause is so important that it can be considered part of the subject itself. Because of that, it should not be set off with two commas.

Here's another way to say this: If the subject of the main clause is clear and easy to identify without the embedded information, surround the embedded clause with two commas. If the embedded information is needed to make sense of the subject of the main clause, don't use any commas.

Let's look at a few more examples before you do the exercises. Make a decision about each of the following sentences. Two commas or none? Take your time.

(a) My parents who are worried about everything going just right should start planning their trip abroad as early as possible.

(b) Travelers who are worried about everything going just right should start planning their trip abroad as early as possible.

(c) My very best friend who loves to find old dishes at bargain prices would really go for this store.

(d) Anyone who loves to find old dishes at bargain prices would really go for this store.

Examples (a) and (c) each require two commas. Examples (b) and (d) should have no commas. It's important to realize that in (a) and (c) you're not using the embedded information to identify the subject of the main clause. In other words, it's not as if you have two or more sets of parents and you want to be sure that the reader knows you're referring to the particular set of parents who are going on a trip soon. The same goes for (c): No matter what he or she loves to find at bargain prices, you have only one very best friend. The subjects *My parents* and *My very best friend* are clear and specific without the embedded information that follows them.

An Important Reminder

Remember, when you drop out the embedded information, you are trying to see whether it is needed or not needed in order to make sense of the subject. You are not trying to see how important the embedded clause is in relationship to the overall meaning of the sentence. Keep your eyes on the *subject* of the main clause!

Exercise 3.2

Draw a wavy line below the embedded clause in each sentence and write *s* over the subject of the main clause. Then make your decision to insert either *two commas* or *none*.

1. St. Nicholas who was a fourth-century bishop in Asia Minor is the patron saint of children and sailors.

2. The dog who guarded the gates of Hades in ancient mythology was the three-headed Cerberus.

3. Janet Reno who became U.S. Attorney General shortly before the cult-related tragedy in Texas was praised for her wilingness to take responsibility for her decisions.

4. The person who wrote the Oz books probably remains unknown even to many of the biggest fans of his work. (The Oz series was written by L. Frank Baum.)

5. The average child who is between two and three years of age does not really know how to play with other children.

The Difference between *Which* and *That*

When a sentence contains an embedded clause beginning with *which,* it usually calls for two commas because *which* is normally used with extra information that is not needed to make the subject clear and specific.

When an embedded clause begins with *that,* the information in the clause is usually needed to understand the subject, so no commas are used. Study these examples:

(a) Neverland, **which is often mistakenly called "Never-Never Land,"** is the place where the children in *Peter Pan* met mermaids, pirates, and Indians.

(b) The lines **that connect points of equal barometric pressure** on a map are isobars.

The Relative Pronoun *Whose*

The relative pronoun *whose* works the same way as *who;* in other words, whose is sometimes used with two commas and sometimes with none. It all depends upon whether or not the embedded clause is needed to make sense of the subject of the main clause.

Better Sentence-Writing

In the previous exercise, you worked only with the embedding word *who.* Now you'll begin to analyze sentences that have been made with *who, whose, which,* and *that.*

Exercise 3.3

Draw a wavy line below the embedded clause in each sentence and write *s* over the subject of the main clause. Then make your decision to insert either *two commas* or *none.* (Remember to think about how important the embedded information is in relation to the *subject of the main clause*—not in relation to the whole sentence.)

1. A person who was born under the sign of Taurus is supposedly stubborn and independent.

2. The person who founded Vassar College was a brewer. (It was Matthew Vassar.)

3. The U.S. Senate which has been called "the most exclusive club in the world" is never open to more than 100 members.

4. The grape that makes California's most successful white wine is the Chardonnay.

5. The abbreviation *lb.* which means pound comes from the Latin word *libra,* meaning "scales."

Exercise 3.4

Here are five pairs of sentences about figures in the history of popular music. Take each pair and embed the (b) sentence into the (a) sentence. (You learned to do this in Chapter 2.) After you have combined the sentences by embedding, decide

3.2 Using Commas in Embedded Sentences

whether to add *two commas* or *none*. You will choose from the relative pronouns *who, whose, which,* and *that.*

1. (a) Chubby Checker worked as a chicken plucker in a poultry shop before he became famous for doing "The Twist."
   (b) His real name was Ernest Evans.

   _____

   _____

   _____

2. (a) Neil Sedaka made a comeback in the 1970s with the help of Elton John.
   (b) He had enjoyed a great deal of success as a songwriter and singer in the 1950s.

   _____

   _____

   _____

3. (a) Critic Jon Landau is responsible for the line "I saw rock 'n' roll's future, and its name is Bruce Springsteen."
   (b) He wrote a rave review after seeing "the Boss" in concert in 1974.

   _____

   _____

   _____

4. (a) Annie Mae Bullock changed her name to Tina Turner.
   (b) She married Ike Turner in 1958.

   _____

   _____

   _____

5. (a) The heart attack occurred while the famous soul singer was performing on stage in Cherry Hill, New Jersey, on September 25, 1975.

(b) It left Jackie Wilson in a coma for the rest of his life.

_____

_____

_____

· ·
3.3 Using Commas to Set Off Phrases
· ·

To understand the punctuation featured in Unit 3, you need to know the difference between a *clause* and a *phrase*. Remember that a clause has both a subject and a verb. A phrase, on the other hand, is a sequence of words that has some sort of meaning but does not have both a subject and a predicate. A phrase might have a noun or a pronoun, or it might have a verb, but it will not have a subject and a verb working together. A phrase might be short or long, but it does less grammatically than a clause.

Label each sentence of words *cl* (for clause) or *p* (for phrase):

1. _____ this man loved his child

2. _____ loving his child

3. _____ the water is deep

4. _____ in a certain depth of water

5. _____ closing the store soon

6. _____ devoted to the exploration of space

7. _____ if we expect to continue the quest

8. _____ expecting to continue the quest

The clauses are items 1, 3 and 7. The phrases are items 2, 4, 5, 6 and 8.

Introductory Phrases

Read this sentence aloud:

Not leaving a thing to chance one cookbook says that Grandma's "pinch" is really one-eighth of a teaspoon.

If you're like most readers, this sentence cannot be read easily without a very short pause and a slight shift in vocal pitch after the word *chance*. Insert a comma after *chance* and read the sentence aloud again. It's clearer with the comma, isn't it? Most writers would insert a comma after *chance* even if they know very little about the formal rules of punctuation. You might say it's a commonsense comma. The reason it's so helpful is that it separates what is called an *introductory phrase* from the independent clause that follows it. Go back to the sentence and draw a bracket over *Not leaving a thing to chance;* then write *introductory phrase* above the bracket. Finally, mark the main parts of the sentence's independent clause.

End Phrases

Now read this sentence aloud:

Kurt Vonnegut has written some of the funniest and saddest books of the twentieth century repeatedly lamenting the exchange of kindness and love for progress and technology.

Go back and insert a comma after the word *century;* then read the sentence aloud once more. Again, it's easier to handle with the comma, isn't it? With the Kurt Vonnegut sentence, we have an example of an *end phrase*. In this kind of sentence, we have the independent clause first. For the convenience of your reader, the end phrase that follows the clause should be set off with a comma. Bracket and label the end phrase in the example sentence and mark the key parts of the independent clause.

Better Sentence-Writing

Notes to Remember

Sometimes it's a matter of your own judgment whether or not to set off an introductory phrase or an end phrase from an independent clause. You'll do fine as long as you use this question as your guideline: *What will make my sentence easier to read?* That, of course, is the whole purpose of punctuation—making your writing easier for your reader to understand.

When a single word or a very short phrase appears before an independent clause, you can *usually* go either way. For example, you can insert a comma after the introductory phrase in each of these sentences, or you can leave it out:

(a) In a minute she'll be ready.

(b) Later he'll stop at the library.

(c) Actually I don't know what to do.

But there are times when you should definitely use a comma even though you might have only *one word* before the start of the independent clause. *Yes, No, First, Second,* and *Third* are good examples of single words that should be set off with a comma when they appear as the first word in a sentence. Another example is a person's name when you are addressing that person in a sentence. Add commas to these sentences:

1. No he isn't scheduled to play tonight.

2. Yes she seems to be the front-runner.

3. First you must have the desire to write well.

4. Second a certain amount of time must be set aside for the effort.

5. Ann come here for a minute.

6. George do you think we'll have time for a short drive?

When in doubt, try reading aloud and let your reader's need for a pause be your guide.

Exercise 3.5

Add commas to set off phrases where doing so makes the sentence easier to read. (You might want to label the key structural components of the clauses to make your decisions easier.)

1. In the lingo of the racetrack a maiden is a horse that has not yet won its first race.

2. First awarded in the American Revolution the Purple Heart is bestowed upon soldiers who are wounded in the line of duty.

3. The city of St. Petersburg has undergone something of an identity crisis through the years having been known both as Petrograd and Leningrad.

4. England adopted a national policy of women's suffrage in 1918 followed by the United States in 1920.

5. The word *khaki* comes from the Persian word *khak* meaning "dust."

Mid Phrases

We've been working with phrases that come before or after an independent clause, but a phrase can also appear in the middle of a clause. When it does, again you have to use your judgment to decide if it should be set off with commas. If you think that a pause and a shift in vocal pitch are required, then use *two commas*—one before and one after the phrase. Read these sentences aloud and notice how helpful the sets of commas are.

(a) The new shopping district, in spite of careful planning by the town council, did not turn out to be much of a success.

(b) Your cousin, with or without his Doberman pinscher, is not welcome here today.

(c) The real reason for her actions will, however, become obvious by the end of the story.

(d) The hospital, surprising everyone, became the center for heart transplant surgery in the region.

3.4 Using Commas in a Series

One of the most natural uses of the comma is for separating items in a series. The items might be three or more of almost anything—nouns, adjectives, verbs, prepositional phrases, or practically any other grammatical unit.

The comma before the *and* that joins the last two items in a series is optional, but it often makes a sentence easier to read if you put it in.

Exercise 3.6

Add commas where they are necessary or helpful for separating items in a series. (Commas that are necessary for other reasons have already been added for you.)

1. Animals that form monogamous bonds between males and females include ducks swans geese eagles foxes wolves and mountain lions.

2. *Fly patterns flares bombs safety blitzes* and *flea flickers* are all part of the lingo known only to the true football fan.

3. The Arc de Triomphe in Paris is 164 feet high 148 feet wide and 72 feet thick.

4. In one of the many works written about him, the famous Faust exchanged his soul for 24 years of wisdom wealth power and pleasure.

5. Until recently, Ariel Miranda Oberon Titania and Umbriel were thought to be the only moons that revolved around the planet Uranus.

Commas in Adjective Pairs

A related rule concerns the use of a comma between two adjectives that describe the same noun. Sometimes you insert a comma, and sometimes you don't. What's the rule? It's really very simple. Just ask yourself if you could put the word *and* between the two adjectives. If you could, then insert the comma. If the word *and* would sound odd between the adjectives, then leave out the comma.

With this guideline in mind, put a comma between the adjectives in one of these two sentences:

1. Peter is a **happy young** man.

2. Peter is an **enthusiastic energetic** man.

The comma should be inserted in sentence 2, right? You know that it's 2 because you might easily say, "Peter is an enthusiastic and energetic man," but you would never say, "Peter is a happy and young man."

This rule can be explained in another way, which you might find useful. Normally, if you can switch the order of the adjectives, then you put in the comma. If you can't switch the order, then you omit the comma. See if this rule works by rewriting sentences 1 and 2, switching the order of *happy* and *young* in sentence 1 and *enthusiastic* and *energetic* in sentence 2:

1. _____

2. _____

When the adjectives in sentence 1 are switched, the sentence—*Peter is a young happy man*—sounds odd, doesn't it? It's not a sentence you'd be likely to write. That tells you to leave out the comma. When the adjectives in sentence 2 are switched, the sentence sounds fine; that tells you to put in the comma.

Exercise 3.7

Underline the adjectives in each sentence. Then insert a comma between them where one is needed. In each set of sentences, one adjective pair will call for a comma, and one will not. Use one or both of the methods just described to help you.

1. (a) She was known for her quick little smile.
   (b) She was known for her generous good-hearted smile.

2. (a) This is a serious military affair.
   (b) This is a ridiculous tragic affair.

3. (a) The garden was bordered with perfect tea roses.
   (b) The garden was bordered with delicate delightful roses.

4. (a) A creamy buttery soup was served in the cafeteria.
   (b) A delicious bean soup was served in the cafeteria.

5. (a) He was a skillful thoughtful sculptor.
   (b) He was a thoughtful Italian sculptor.

3.5 Cumulative Review of Commas

This unit simply allows you to practice all the different comma rules you've learned in this chapter. But before beginning the exercise, please study these two additional rules.

Commas to Set Off City from State

You normally use one comma between the name of a city and a state and another comma after the state. For example:

1. (a) The authors of *The Best* insist that **New York, New York,** is home to the best hamburgers in America.

2. (a) **New Haven, Connecticut,** is the city where they found the best pizza.

The only exception is when the city and state come right before another punctuation mark, such as a period or a semicolon. In these examples, you use only the comma between city and state:

1. (b) The authors of *The Best* insist that the best hamburgers in America are served at the Campus Dining Room Restaurant and Bar in **New York, New York.**

2. (b) Peter Passell and Leonard Ross really liked the pizza at The Spot in **New Haven, Connecticut;** in fact, they called it the best pizza in the United States.

Commas in Dates

The rule for punctuating dates is similar. You use one comma between the day of the month and the year and another comma after the year. In other words, you normally set off the year with two commas, just as you usually set off the state with two commas. For example:

(a) The first use of videotape on television was on **October 23, 1956,** on "The Jonathan Winters Show."

(b) **December 25, 1968,** was the day when the *Apollo 8* astronauts became the first human beings to see the far side of the moon.

The same exception that applies to city and state applies here; in other words, you use no comma after the year if another punctuation mark is used in that position.

Exercise 3.8

Add commas where they are necessary or helpful, according to the guidelines of this chapter.

1. If you ever really want to go to Timbuktu you'll have to head out for Mali in northwest Africa. Timbuktu which was a famous center for trading in gold was settled by the Tuaregs in 1087.

2. The ice-cream sundae now a classic American treat was supposedly created in a Wisconsin ice-cream parlor and originally it was served only on Sundays.

3. On October 25 1940 Col. B.O. Davis became the first African-American to attain the rank of brigader general in U.S. military history.

4. For concocting the original Coca-Cola in 1886 John Styth Pemberton an Atlanta pharmacist will always be remembered and appreciated.

5. When fireflies light up they send sexual signals to one another. According to the experts male and female fireflies identify themselves and indicate sexual interest by the frequency and intensity of their flashes.

6. King Louis XIV of France who was a ballet dancer from the time he was 13 years old is credited with founding the Royal Ballet Company.

7. A desert rose is not a rose at all. It's a rock that is made up of fused eroded grains of sand. Desert roses which are "flowers" carved by the elements are not difficult to find in the Sahara.

8. The first person to be called the "father" of his country was Cicero not George Washington.

9. Totally unrelated to either sweets or bread a sweetbread is actually the thymus gland of an animal.

10. The longest heaviest snake in the world is the South American anaconda or python a typical specimen measuring 30 feet or more.

3.6 Using Semicolons

The basic function of the semicolon (;) is simple. A semicolon is used where you could use a capital letter and a period, but you'd rather not have such a strong break between your clauses. It's good for spots where you want to bring clauses together, but you don't want to use a conjunction.

In other words, a semicolon is used between independent clauses that are not linked by a conjunction. A semicolon is used when the information in the independent clauses is related or balanced. Here are five good examples for you to study:

1. Children between the ages of one and three need about 25 grams of protein a day; adults need 55 to 75 grams a day.

2. The red parts of poinsettias are not flowers; the red parts are actually leaves.

3. A female has two X chromosomes; a male has one X chromosome and one Y chromosome.

71

4. The first president who didn't go to college was George Washington; the last was Harry Truman.

5. It is against federal law to impersonate a 4-H Club member; it is also a federal offense to misuse the 4-H symbol in a fraudulent manner.

Label the kernels of the clauses in examples (1) through (5) if that helps you see that each sentence is made up of two independent clauses. Note that the first word after the semicolon is not capitalized unless it is a proper noun.

Exercise 3.9

Insert one semicolon into each sentence. Label the key parts of the clauses if you need to. (In this exercise and in other exercises in this unit, any punctuation that is not related to the use of the semicolon is already supplied. See sentence 4, for example.)

1. Mildred "Babe" Didrikson was voted the woman athlete of the year in 1932 for her accomplishments in track she received the honor for her achievements in golf in 1954.

2. The Eiffel Tower was not intended as a permanent structure it was built as a temporary attraction for the Paris Exposition in 1889.

3. The skeletons of sharks are not composed of bone they are made up entirely of cartilage.

4. According to one national survey by *American Demographics,* high school boys expected a starting salary of $18,500 for their first full-time job high school girls expected a starting salary of only $14,700.

5. In the 1870s the most admired American sports heroes were riflemen oarsmen were almost as popular with the U.S. public.

An Introductory Word or Phrase for the Clause After the Semicolon

You know that semicolons are used when a writer wants to show a relationship between two independent clauses. (Sometimes it's actually independent *combinations* of clauses; for example, you might have a complex sentence on one side of a semicolon and a compound sentence on the other side.) Often a writer uses an introductory word or phrase at the beginning of the clause that follows the semicolon. *This word or phrase does not connect the clauses. The semicolon does that.* The introductory word or phrase simply makes the relationship between the clauses clearer and more explicit.

Here's a list of words and phrases that are often used in this way. They're divided into groups on the basis of having similar or closely related meanings:

for example	therefore
for instance	consequently
however	as a result
on the other hand	in fact
nevertheless	as a matter of fact
also	actually
furthermore	then
in addition	now
in other words	later

Better Sentence-Writing

Here's a sample sentence:

According to one national survey by *American Demographics,* high school boys expected a starting salary of $18,500 for their first full-time job; high school girls expected a starting salary of only $14,700.

The sentence is perfectly fine the way it is. But it can be revised in a very small way so that the contrast it describes is more obvious. To see how this works, fill in the blank with an introductory word or phrase from the list above:

According to one national survey by *American Demographics,* high school boys expected a starting salary of $18,500 for their first full-time job; _____, high school girls expected a starting salary of only $14,700.

If you chose *however* or *on the other hand,* you're correct. Either one helps to make the contrast between the clauses more apparent.

Notice that a comma is used after the introductory word or phrase. This is the normal procedure: Use a semicolon before the introductory word or phrase and a comma after it.

Other Introductory Words and Phrases

The list we have given you is certainly not complete, but it's a good basic list of introductory words that can be used in creating this particular sentence structure. But there are many other expressions that can serve as introductory words and phrases before a clause. You'll probably come up with a variety in your own writing. Look at these two examples:

(a) The manager of a professional baseball team can visit the pitcher on the mound only once; *after that*, he can't go out again unless he's going to call in a reliever.

(b) There are many legends about the Canary Islands; *according to one*, the islands are really the highest peaks of Atlantis, the lost continent.

Exercise 3.10

Punctuate these sentences with semicolons and commas. Some sentences call for a semicolon only, and others call for a semicolon and a comma. (Label the key parts of clauses if you need to.)

1. The largest lake or inland sea in the world is the Caspian Sea however the biggest freshwater lake is Lake Superior.

2. The familiar word *oriental* refers to the people and culture of the East the less familiar word *occidental* refers to the people and culture of the West.

3. Fyodor Dostoyevsky wrote a novel called *The Gambler* in fact the great Russian literary figure was himself a compulsive gambler.

4. North America is slowly moving westward at an annual rate of about three inches consequently the Atlantic Ocean is now about 20 feet wider than it was when Columbus crossed it.

5. During the ninth-century reign of Alfred, King of the West Saxons, there was a specific punishment for practically every bodily injury for example if a person's thigh were pierced, he or she could collect a fine of 30 shillings from the injuring party.

6. A copyright stays in effect for the lifetime of the creator of the copyrighted work in fact it is valid for his or her lifetime plus 50 years.

7. In O. Henry's "The Gift of the Magi," a husband sells his watch in order to buy his wife a pair of combs for her beautiful hair the wife cuts off her long hair and sells it in order to buy her husband a fob chain for his watch.

8. Much of Humphrey Bogart's mystique came as a result of his wonderful performance in *Casablanca* however few people know that Ronald Reagan was originally cast as Rick, the main character.

9. An amulet is an object that supposedly protects a person against bad luck a talisman is something that is thought to attract good luck.

10. A wolf's eye, a stone with a hole in it, and a horseshoe are examples of amulets a four-leaf clover and a rabbit's foot are examples of talismans.

A Note of Caution

There's one bad habit that some writers fall into. They begin to assume that the introductory words and phrases listed earlier are always used with semicolons and are never used in any other ways in a sentence. Of course, that's not true. These words and phrases are not used with a semicolon unless an independent clause (or an independent combination of clauses) appears both before and after the semicolon. All these words and phrases can be used with semicolons, but they can all be used in other spots in sentences, too. Study these correct examples and then complete Exercise 3.11:

1. (a) Craig always has something to complain about; *for instance,* he might be upset about lumpy mashed potatoes one night and the growing national debt the next.
   (b) Craig's complaints, *for instance,* cover everything from lumpy mashed potatoes to the growing national debt.

2. (a) The doctor predicted a good outcome for the operation; *as a matter of fact,* she almost guaranteed total recovery.
   (b) The doctor's prediction, *as a matter of fact,* was almost totally optimistic.

Remember, there are no words or phrases that are always used with semicolons. All of these introductory words and phrases, can be used in other ways in sentences. They don't always signal the need for a semicolon.

Exercise 3.11

Punctuate the following sentences. Some sentences call for no additional punctuation, some for commas only, and some for a semicolon and a comma.

1. (a) Robert had a great idea.
   (b) His idea however was not immediately accepted by the group.
   (c) Robert had a great idea however it was not immediately accepted by the group.

2. (a) Christina was more than a passing acquaintance of Ben's in fact she was his closest friend.
   (b) Christina was very close to Ben.
   (c) She was in fact his best friend in the world.

3. (a) Mitchell wants to graduate with a degree in mechanical engineering at the end of his college days.
   (b) This highly motivated young man is therefore going to have to work hard and play little during the next four years.
   (c) Mitchell wants to graduate from college with a degree in mechanical engineering therefore he is going to have to work and play little during the next four years.

4. (a) The exact time that language skills emerge in children varies greatly among individuals.

(b) Language skills emerge at greatly varying times in the development of children for example some toddlers begin talking in short sentences around the age of two.

(c) Other completely normal youngsters for example speak very little until they're three.

5. (a) John and Marsha are debating whether they should go with periwinkle blue or China red for their new carpet.

(b) Marsha thinks periwinkle blue would be an elegant choice on the other hand John is afraid that blue might make the room seem cold.

(c) John on the other hand thinks that China red would be warm and lively.

• •
3.7 Using Colons
• •

Occasionally, you might want to use a colon (:) to set up a list. In order to do this, you need to create a complete sentence, usually one that ends with a subject complement or a direct object.

Don't do this:

The four major reasons for the landslide victory *were:* the candidate's personal popularity, the enthusiastic support of his party, his stand on budget issues, and the general mood of the nation.

What's wrong with it? The problem is that the colon follows a verb—in this sentence, the verb *were.* You might see this type of sentence in a newspaper or a popular magazine, but it's not accepted in academic writing by most college teachers.

78

In academic writing, it is normally expected that a subject complement or a direct object should appear before the colon. Label the complement in this example:

The four major reasons for the landslide victory were obvious: the candidate's personal popularity, the enthusiastic support of his party, his stand on budget issues, and the general mood of the nation.

If you identified the word *obvious* as the subject complement, you're correct. The addition of *obvious* in the second sentence corrects the problem that exists in the first sentence. A colon should not follow a verb.

An Important Note

Sometimes you'll use a word that isn't a complement or a direct object but that still gives the sentence a sense of completion before the items in the list begin. For example, let's look at this correct sentence:

The strange coincidences happened during each of these years: 1921, 1937, 1952, 1964, and 1986.

You know that the word *years* is not the complement of the verb *happened*. If something happened, it happened. We don't ask a question such as "It happened what?" So strictly speaking, *happened* is a verb that doesn't take a complement.

The word *years* is not a complement or a direct object, but it does help to give the first part of the sentence a sense of completion—a sense that now we've finished the setup, and we're ready to present the items in the list.

To keep things simple, we'll refer to this kind of word as the *complement of the setup*. In the majority of sentences—your own and ours—you'll be working with a true complement anyway, so this won't often be an issue.

The important thing is this: You need a feeling of completeness in the setup, the part of the sentence that precedes the colon. That sense of wholeness in the setup can be produced by using a *true complement or a complement-type word*.

Exercise 3.12

Punctuate the following sentences with colons and commas. Some sentences might call for commas only. Label the subject complement *sub com* and the direct object *do* to help you see if a sentence has the setup needed for a colon. (Punctuation not related to this unit has already been supplied.)

1. In *The Misunderstood Child,* Dr. Larry B. Silver says that the human brain goes through major growth spurts during five time periods. Those periods are the following between three and ten months between two and four years between six and eight years between 10 and 12 years and between 14 and 16 years.

2. Santa's eight tiny reindeer are Dasher Dancer Prancer Vixen Comet Cupid Donner and Blitzen.

3. These are the seven wonders of the ancient world the Great Pyramid of Cheops the Hanging Gardens of Babylon the Tomb of King Mausolus at Halicarnassus the Temple of Artemis the Colossus of Rhodes the Statue of Zeus at Olympia and the lighthouse on the Isle of Pharos.

4 Most of us would probably call a flock of birds a flock of birds. But those who want to be more precise might use one of these terms a bevy of quail a muster of peacocks a charm of finches or an exaltation of larks.

5. Charles Blondin, the French acrobat and tightrope walker, crossed Niagara Falls in 1855 1859 and 1860.

A Common Error

One very common error is to use a colon after the word *including* or after *such as*. These situations, however, do not call for colons. The word *including* or the expression *such as* is really better viewed as the start of an "end phrase" or, in other words, a phrase following a clause. Look at these correct examples:

(a) J.B. Rhine of Duke University has conducted scientific studies of various aspects of parapsychology, **including** clairvoyance, extrasensory perception, psychokinesis, and telepathy.

(b) J.B. Rhine of Duke University has conducted scientific studies of various aspects of parapsychology, **such as** clairvoyance, extrasensory perception, psychokinesis, and telepathy.

You should *not* use a colon in (a) and (b). Try rewriting the sentence about J.B. Rhine so that a colon is appropriate. Then punctuate sentences 1 through 4:

1. These are the seven deadly sins anger covetousness envy gluttony lust pride and sloth.

2. He committed each and every one of the seven deadly sins anger covetousness envy gluttony lust pride and sloth.

3. She committed a number of the seven deadly sins including anger envy lust and sloth.

4. Of the seven deadly sins, they had their own personal favorites such as gluttony lust and sloth.

1. sins: anger, covetousness, envy, gluttony, lust, pride, and sloth; 2. sins: anger, covetousness, envy, gluttony, lust, pride, and sloth; 3. sins, including anger, envy, lust, and sloth; 4. favorites, such as gluttony, lust, and sloth.

Another Use for the Colon

There is another way to use the colon, but if you still have difficulty with *any* of the other rules of punctuation, you should skip this brief section. This is a low priority compared with the other rules, and it will *not* be included in the cumulative exercises in the next unit. But for many writers, it is a valuable sentence-combining technique, so that is way we are presenting it here.

The colon can be used in this way:

Carol Tavris's *The Measure of Women* has an interesting

subtitle: *Why Women Are Not the Better Sex, the Inferior*

Sex, or the Opposite Sex.

Mark the key parts of the clause before the colon. You see that we do have a complement—*subtitle*—just as we always have a complement when we are using the colon before a list. But here we're not setting up for a list; we're setting up for an *explanation of the word in the subject complement or direct object position.* The word *subtitle* is explained by the words that follow the colon.

When you make this kind of a sentence, you can capitalize the first word after the colon if the explanation is a full sentence. If you use the capitalization option, be consistent within a piece of writing.

3.8 Cumulative Review of Commas, Semicolons, and Colons

This unit contains exercises that ask you to use all the information you've learned and all the skills you've acquired in Chapter 3.

A Few Important Words About the Exercises

In these exercises, you will be using *commas, colons,* and *semicolons.* Commas, of course, will be used most frequently because the comma has so many different functions. But not every exercise will call for all three punctuation marks. And some sentences will call for no additional punctuation.

Furthermore, some sentences will lend themselves to more than one interpretation or more than one method of punctuation.

If punctuation is needed to introduce a direct quote, it will be supplied for you. You'll learn how to punctuate quotes in the next chapter.

Label the key parts of clauses if that practice is helpful to you.

Finally, *mark up the book!* Most often, if you take a look at the books of students who are really improving in their writing, you find that those books are completely marked up with notes, labels, underlinings, and symbols. The marks give testimony to a lot of hard work and show that those students are making the information their own. Develop a system—whether it's circling conjunctions, drawing wavy lines under embedded clauses, or whatever—and use it. And when you're stuck on a particular sentence, if you can't figure it out, put a question mark in the margin and move on. You can come back to it later.

Exercise 3.13

Insert commas, semicolons, and colons where they are needed.

1. *Sea of Slaughter* which was published by Atlantic Monthly Press was written by Farley Mowat.

2. Mowat who is a Canadian is a naturalist and a writer.

3. Focusing on the northern part of the Atlantic seaboard Mowat examines the history of man's relationship with wildlife since the first Europeans arrived on this continent.

4. Although Farley Mowat's research is limited to one geographical area his conclusions can be said to hold true for the entire continent of North America.

5. According to the author human beings have meant almost nothing but death for the mammals birds and fish of North America in fact Mowat estimates that the entire "biomass" has been reduced by perhaps as much as 95 percent through human destruction.

6. Animals have been "overkilled" basically for three reasons economic recreational and scientific.

7. Economic reasons include the killing of animals for meat hides and fur.

8. Some species have survived but they have survived only with great difficulty for example the wolf the Plains buffalo and the grizzly bear were depleted by the millions because of wanton slaughter by human beings.

9. Other animals such as the passenger pigeon the sea mink and the Eastern buffalo are gone forever driven into extinction by the planet's supposedly most intelligent creatures.

10. These are harsh tragic realities and they are not only a matter of history animals continue to die for sport for fashion for food and for experimentation.

Exercise 3.14

Insert commas, semicolons, and colons where they are needed.

1. *Sea of Slaughter* a substantial book of more than 400 pages points out that human beings destroy their own rich history when they destroy any part of the natural world.

2. Many people for example believe that the great auk was only a myth.

3. Farley Mowat assures us that this fascinating bird which could dive to a depth of 300 feet and stay underwater for a quarter of an hour did exist.

4. While the great auk once numbered 100 million its natural enemies numbered only one.

5. That enemy of course was deadly it was man.

6. Mowat also reminds us that the whale once one of the most stable of all life forms is now in danger of disappearing from the planet.

7. The author sees only one animal that has succeeded in thriving against all odds the coyote.

8. Mowat credits the coyote for being adaptable and just plain smart.

9. Lamenting man's role as a predator Mowat concludes that there is some hope for the future but the best hope lies with aware and sensitive individuals not with massive organizations.

10. Although books like *Sea of Slaughter* are rare they can make important headway in forming sensitive aware human beings. As Robert W. Smith said in a review of Mowat's publication it "deserves to stand with Rachel Carson's *Silent Spring* as an outstanding indictment of man's stupidity in alienating himself from nature."

Chapter 4

Revising Sentences

••

4.1 Dangling Modifiers
••

In Chapter 3, you learned to punctuate sentences that have *introductory phrases*. In this unit, you'll learn to make sure that the introductory phrase that you set off with a comma really describes what it's supposed to describe—the subject of the main clause or the action of the subject. If the introductory phrase modifies some other word in the sentence (or a word that doesn't even appear in the sentence), then the introductory phrase is called a *dangling modifier*. A sentence that has a dangling modifier is a weak, awkward, illogical-sounding sentence.

Here's an example:

1. **Employed as a weekend weatherman on an Indianapolis TV** station, hailstones as big as canned hams were once predicted by David Letterman.

The subject of the sentence is the word *hailstones*. Whatever introductory phrase is attached to the sentence before the subject must describe the subject or the action of the subject. But the modifier in sentence 1 obviously is supposed to describe

David Letterman, not hailstones or anything that hailstones could do. To see if an introductory phrase is well attached or if it's dangling, ask yourself a question like this: Can the word *hailstones* (your subject) be described as *employed as a weekend weatherman on an Indianapolis TV station* (your introductory phrase)? If it can, then you're okay. If it can't, then you have a dangling modifier.

Once you know you have a dangling modifier, there is usually more than one good way of revising it. Here are some possible correct rewrites for sentence 1:

(a) Employed as a weekend weatherman on an Indianapolis TV station, David Letterman once predicted hailstones as big as canned hams.

(b) David Letterman, who once worked as a weekend weatherman on an Indianapolis TV station, predicted hailstones as big as canned hams.

(c) Hailstones as big as canned hams were once predicted by an Indianapolis TV station's weekend weatherman, who was none other than David Letterman.

Exercise 4.1

Label each item *OK* or *DM* (dangling modifier). Underline the introductory modifier and label the subject *S* before you make your decision. Then rewrite the sentences that contain dangling modifiers; try to use a variety of sentence-combining techniques as you do your rewrites. Use your own paper, please. (The information here is found in *Life-spans, Or, How Long Things Last,* by Frank Kendig and Richard Hutton.)

1. _____ Refrigerated at the proper temperature, beer can be stored a maximum of three months; after that, it often has a buttery or papery taste.

2. ＿＿＿ Wrapped individually in plastic or foil, hard candies and caramels can last anywhere from three to twelve months at room temperature.

3. ＿＿＿ Cared for properly, the U.S. Army estimates that an M-1 rifle should last 10,000 rounds.

4. ＿＿＿ Currently about four to five billion years old, scientists believe that the sun has a life span of 10 billion years.

5. ＿＿＿ Performed upon average skin, plastic surgeons estimate that a successful face lift should last from six to 10 years.

Exercise 4.2

Label each item *OK* or *DM*. Underline introductory modifiers and label subjects. Rewrite problem sentences on your own paper. (These tidbits are from *Joan Embery's Collection of Amazing Animal Facts.*)

1. ＿＿＿ Weighing up to 32 ounces, Southeast Asia is the home of the world's largest bat, whose wingspan has been measured at five feet, seven inches.

2. ＿＿＿ Having no bark at all, the basenji dog of Africa makes the perfect hunting dog.

3. ＿＿＿ Extremely long-lived, it is known that swans can survive up to one hundred years.

4. ＿＿＿ Thought to be the heaviest insect in the world, the goliath beetle, which can weigh almost a quarter of a pound, has been observed peeling a banana while in captivity.

5. ＿＿＿ Lacking the tiger's usual reddish orange coloring, some zoos have black and white Bengal tigers, all

of whom are descendants of a single white male tiger named Bohan, who was found in a jungle in India around the middle of this century.

• •
4.2 Faulty Parallelism
• •

If you've ever been told that your writing is sometimes awkward in spots, one problem might be *faulty parallelism.* Usually when you're writing about a series of things within one sentence, each item in the series should be in the same form as the other items. If the items are in the same form, you have parallelism in your writing. If they are not in the same form, you have faulty parallelism, and that's the problem we're going to work on in this unit.

When we talk about items being in the same form, we're talking about grammatical forms, such as nouns, verbs, adjectives, adverbs, prepositional phrases, and clauses. Here is an example of faulty parallelism in which it is easy to see that the writer is switching grammatical forms:

(a) In order to be classified as great, a baseball player must hit with power, a high lifetime batting average is necessary, to field well, be a fast runner, and throwing with strength and precision.

After you read (a) aloud, do the same with (b), which is a good example of parallelism:

(b) In order to be classified as great, a baseball player must hit with power, achieve a high lifetime batting average, field well, run fast, and throw with strength and precision.

Just by reading it aloud, you can tell that (b) has a nice sound, a flow, a repeated pattern that (a) lacks. By analyzing the structure of (b), you can see that the sentence has those good features because all the parts match in form and because all of them can be read with what we call a "setup." The setup in (b) is *a baseball player must*. Notice that each of the five items can be read fluently with *a baseball player must*. Read aloud each of the following items with this setup:

a baseball player must:

1. hit with power

2. achieve a high lifetime batting average

3. field well

4. run fast

5. throw with strength and precision

In other words, each item in the series (1 through 5) can be read individually with the setup, which in this case is *a baseball player must*. In sentence (b) the setup is the subject plus a helping verb, and the items all begin with base verbs *(hit, achieve, field, run, and throw)*.

In your rewrite of sentence (a), what if you had repeated the word must five times? Then you'd have this: *In order to be classified as great, a baseball player must hit with power, must achieve a high lifetime batting average, must field well, must run fast, and must throw with strength and precision.* It sounds a little stiff and wordy, doesn't it? It shows one of the problems you might encounter in your rewrites. Your revisions of sentences that contain faulty parallelism should normally cut down on wordiness, not add to it. Therefore, you should use a word like *must* only once—in the setup—if you can, and that way you'll avoid awkward, pointless repetition. Use repetition only if you have a special reason for doing so; one valid reason is to give extra emphasis. But this will be the rare case, not the norm.

You should also realize, however, that sentence (b) is not the only possible revision of the faulty parallelism in sentence (a). Here is another, quite different rewrite that is also good:

(c) In order to be classified as great, baseball players have to be more than power hitters with a high lifetime batting average; they must also excel at running, fielding, and throwing.

Notice how sentence (c) has parallel structure by using the parallel verbs *running, fielding,* and *throwing.*

Important Notes on Creating Strong Parallelism

When you try to correct faulty parallelism and to create good parallelism, you'll sometimes find that there's no way you can construct one setup that will work with all your items. That's no problem. In that situation, just create two setups. For instance, you might have written a list of qualities that a person should have to become a good doctor, but mixed in it are a number of observations about characteristics that probably do not predict success in medical practice. What are you going to do? You might unravel your items and create one setup for the "dos," or the *assets,* as you might call them, and another setup for the "don'ts," or the *liabilities.*

Sometimes it's not a matter of creating two setups; rather it is a matter of removing one stubborn item and making it into a separate sentence. That is another good solution for faulty parallelism.

Exercise 4.3

In each of the following items, underline the part that is an example of faulty parallelism. Then rewrite that section, correcting the problem. (You don't have to rewrite the entire item, just the part that needs to be revised.) Try to use a good setup that you can read with all the parts that follow it. Read your revision aloud.

1. One key factor in the effort to revitalize our national system of education is the need to raise the minimum grade point average required for entrance into a college

or university teacher-training program. In addition, if the teachers of the future are to come from the best class of students, they will need higher salaries, the issue of greater professional status being important, and if they have more opportunities for advancement.

_____

_____

_____

2. Some transcontinental travelers have found ways of minimizing their great curse—jet lag. If you're flying from the United States to Europe, for instance, there is no way to avoid this phenomenon because traveling such a long distance in such a short time will inevitably disrupt the body's rhythms. But there are things you can do to adjust as quickly as possible. Seasoned travelers suggest that you take a daytime flight, should eat as little as possible on the plane, and napping as much as you can in the air. Then when you reach your destination, whatever you do, don't go to sleep until the sun sets.

_____

_____

_____

3. Many parents find it difficult to know if a child is ready to start kindergarten. According to Louise Bates Ames and Frances L. Ilg of the Gesell Institute of Child Development, it's not just a matter of chronological age. Not all five-year-olds are ready to benefit from being in an organized school setting. Ames and Ilg suggest that before the child begins, parents should make sure he or she already has certain skills. The child who is ready for kindergarten should be able to name at least three or four colors, drawing or copying a square should be a simple matter, repeat a series of four numbers without practicing them, the ability to tell the

right hand from the left, and if the child can identify what things such as cars, chairs, and shoes are made of. The authors suggest, by the way, that most little ones are not ready for kindergarten until they're five and a half.

_____

_____

_____

4.3 Passive Sentences

Like faulty parallelism, unnecessary passive sentences are a source of awkwardness in the writing of many students.

You know that the word *passive* ordinarily means inactive. People are called passive if they wait for things to happen instead of making them happen. Passive sentences are somewhat similar. A passive sentence is not technically wrong like a run-on or a fragment, but it's relatively weak, flat, and dead. The subject of a passive sentence does not act; it is acted upon.

Here is an example:

1. (a) The position of poet laureate of the United States is currently held by Rita Dove.

Doesn't that sentence sound awkward? Why use the word *position* as the subject? Wouldn't *Rita Dove* be a more natural choice for a subject? After all, she is the one who is doing something. Here's an *active* rewrite of the sentence:

1. (b) Rita Dove currently holds the position of poet laureate of the United States.

Here's another passive sentence:

2. (a) In some of Sir Arthur Conan Doyle's stories, the violin is occasionally played by Sherlock Holmes.

An active rewrite is this:

2. (b) Sherlock Holmes occasionally plays the violin in some of Sir Arthur Conan Doyle's stories.

Acceptable Passive Sentences

Sometimes passive sentences are all right. For instance, it's fine to use a passive sentence if you don't know who did a certain action. For example, it would be perfectly logical to write, "The music was written in the seventeenth century" if you didn't know who composed the piece. Passive sentences might also be written about an anonymous poem, a purse stolen by an unidentified person, and so forth.

Another valid reason for using a passive sentence is the writer's desire to place emphasis on a certain area. For example, look at these sentences, each of which is passive for a good reason:

(a) The pterodactyl, a flying dinosaur, was discovered by O.C. Marsh in 1871.

(b) The ancient city of Troy, which for centuries was thought to be purely mythical, was discovered by Heinrich Schliemann.

In each example, the writer might have thought that the thing discovered—in one case, the pterodactyl and in the other, the city of Troy—was of greater historical importance than the person who discovered it. That value judgment then would have led the writer to put the discovery rather than the discoverer in the subject position. Certainly, another writer, perhaps with a different emphasis in mind, could have made *O.C.*

95

Marsh and *Heinrich Schliemann* the subjects. The point is that it's all right to use a passive sentence if you have a valid reason for it.

Here is one more example of an acceptable passive sentence:

(c) The water in and around Minamata, Japan, had been completely contaminated, and many children from the area were born with severe birth defects as a result of the mercury their mothers had ingested.

The first clause—*The water in and around Minamata, Japan, had been completely contaminated*—is passive, but there may be a good reason for this construction. Perhaps the writer is not concerned at this point with the question of *who* contaminated the water, and wants instead to emphasize the simple fact that the water was contaminated.

Important Notes About Passive Sentences

Before you do the exercises in this unit, you need to realize that the "by so and so" phrase does not always appear in a passive sentence; sometimes it is only implied. Such a sentence might still be in need of a good rewrite.

Sometimes when you are changing a sentence from passive to active, you'll find other opportunities to make it crisper and less wordy.

And sometimes you'll find a sentence that is passive in more than one clause. Make sure you change each passive clause when you revise it.

Finally, you'll notice that all passive sentences are not alike. Read them aloud, and you'll hear that some sound horrible, whereas others barely need to be rewritten or, perhaps, in some cases don't need to be rewritten at all.

The important thing is to eliminate unnecessary passive sentences and to make your writing as active and lively as possible.

Exercise 4.4

Rewrite these passive sentences, making them active. Please use your own paper.

1. Approximately 200 pounds are gained per day by the baby calf of a blue whale.

2. An age of over 80 years has been reached by goldfish in captivity.

3. The practice of monogamy is observed by storks.

4. Its tail is used effectively as a whip by an iguana when it is threatened.

5. One-third of the total amount of canned fish in the United States is eaten by cats.

Exercise 4.5

Rewrite these passive sentences, making them active. Please use our own paper.

1. Their physical senses can be developed by human beings to a much higher degree than most people realize.

2. Enough examples from everyday life can be found by anyone to determine that this is true.

3. For example, the amount of alcohol or acid in a particular wine can be tasted by an experienced vintner to within one percent.

4. Differences between certain shades of red that are indistinguishable to the layperson can be seen by expert color technicians.

5. Just by its feel, the moisture content of bread dough can be measured by some professional bakers to within two percent of accuracy when the dough is being kneaded by them.

4.4 Direct and Indirect Quotes

There are many times, especially in college-level writing, when you work with the words of others. There are two basic ways that you can present what others have said: (1) You can quote a person *directly,* using his. or her exact words, or (2) you can quote *indirectly,* expressing the person's thoughts in your own words. An indirect quote is also called a paraphrase.

A direct quote is a presentation of the exact words that someone used. An indirect quote is a description of what was said.

Here is an example of a *direct quote:*

(a) In a review of Woody Allen's *Hannah and Her Sisters,* critic David Ansen said, "Anyone bemoaning the disappearance of adult matter from the movies need look no farther."

In (a), the writer is choosing to use the exact words that Ansen used in his review. To show that, the writer must enclose what Ansen said within a set of double quotation marks ("). Notice that the word *Anyone* is capitalized. The first word of a direct quote is usually capitalized. (We'll discuss an exception later.)

Below, the writer is choosing to quote Ansen *indirectly:*

(b) In a review of *Hannah and Her Sisters,* critic David Ansen said that anyone who's complaining that adult subject matter has disappeared from the movies doesn't have to look beyond this Woody Allen movie.

Sentence (b) contains an indirect quote, which is also called a paraphrase. In (b), the writer does not use Ansen's exact words but does communicate Ansen's point. When you quote someone indirectly, remember that you still must give the person credit. That's why Ansen's name is used in (b) just as it was in (a).

Punctuating Direct Quotes

In addition to using double quotation marks before and after a person's exact words, you also have to learn to use the correct punctuation to set off the attribution part of the sentence. This is the part that tells who said it; for instance, *he said* and *she remarked* are attributions. Often you use a comma to set off an attribution, sometimes you use a colon, and occasionally you use no punctuation at all.

1. Using a Comma

If the attribution is simply a subject and a verb or verb phrase, use a comma after it. Study these correct examples, in which only a subject and verb appear in each attribution.

She said, "_____."

He commented, "_____."

They insisted, "_____."

An s-v attribution can also appear at the end of the sentence; in other words, it may follow the direct quote. When the attribution is in this position, use a comma before it. Look at these correct examples:

"_____," said Barbara.

"_____," commented the captain.

"_____," they insisted.

When it's appropriate, an attribution can even interrupt a direct quote. For instance, a writer might choose to structure a sentence this way:

"Just once this week," James suggested, "let's try to get through an entire evening without turning on the television."

Better Sentence-Writing

In such sentences, the attribution is set off with two commas. Make sure to enclose each part of the quote within a set of double quotation marks. Use a period and a capital letter only if each of the two sections is a full sentence. This is a correct example:

"He doesn't know what to do," my mother said. "He's completely confused."

2. Using a Colon

If the attribution contains a subject complement or a direct object, use a colon after it. Study these examples and label each with *s, v, sub com,* and *do.*

The waiter gave us some advice: "_____."

She said only three words: "_____."

The lawyer issued one warning: "_____."

3. Using No Punctuation

Occasionally, no punctuation is used directly before a direct quote. Here are two correct examples:

Jack Kroll, the well-known critic, called Henry Fonda, Gary Cooper, Spencer Tracy, and Jimmy Stewart a "celluloid Mount Rushmore of American icons."

A *Washington Post* reviewer once wrote that novelist Gloria Naylor's talent "glows like beaten copper."

Because of the way the quoted material is worked into the sentence, the first word of the direct quote is not capitalized, nor is the quote set off with a comma or colon.

One Last Note

Don't double your punctuation when the attribution comes after a direct quote. In other words, if a direct quote ends with a question mark or an exclamation point, omit the comma. These examples are correct:

"Who's watching the store?" she asked.

"Throw the ball!" they yelled.

Exercise 4.6

Make the necessary changes wherever you find direct quotes. Your changes may involve quotation marks, commas, colons, and capitalization. Some sentences might not contain direct quotes; those sentences should not be changed.

1. Zsa Zsa Gabor once said I'm a wonderful housekeeper. Every time I get a divorce, I keep the house.

2. In 1787, the United States minted a copper coin with a simple motto mind your business.

3. *The Outer Limits*, a science fiction TV series, always opened with the same line there is nothing wrong with your set.

4. Assassination is the extreme form of censorship claimed George Bernard Shaw, the famous playwright.

5. George Gallup, the nationally known pollster, once said that he could prove the existence of God statistically.

Chapter 5

Free Exercises in Sentence Combining

This is an important chapter for everyone, no matter what your strengths and weaknesses are. The exercises in Chapter 5 will help you reinforce the skills you've learned to this point and assist you in gaining greater flexibility and variety in your sentence structure.

The chapter contains a series of sentence-combining exercises to do on your own paper. In terms of sentence structure, sentence combining is a great finishing touch. You've learned a lot of dos and don'ts, and this is an excellent way of reviewing and exercising them. If you've had a hard time with run-ons or comma splices, for example, this chapter will give you another opportunity to work on correcting them. You'll also get more practice reworking sentences with fragments, dangling modifiers, and faulty parallelism. After all, these errors are nothing more than missteps in the process of sentence combining. And if you've had any difficulty making compound, complex, or embedded sentences, or remembering the rules for punctuating them correctly, the exercises in this chapter will help you. If you need more work on semicolons and colons, try to use them whenever you think they're appropriate.

Now let's examine how free sentence-combining exercises work. Please read the following series of sentences carefully.

Better Sentence-Writing

Agatha Christie disappeared in 1924.

She was a famous English mystery writer.

She was missing for 10 days.

Her disappearance made headlines in the British newspapers.

It made the front page.

If these five sentences appeared consecutively in a college student's paper, they would be judged to have a choppy, overly simple sound. On the other hand, if they appeared in the writing of a 10-year-old, they probably would be regarded quite favorably. Adult writers generally use short, unconnected sentences infrequently, and when they do, it's for a dramatic effect. Normally, adult writers are interested in showing relationships between facts, and that's why they automatically combine clauses most of the time. Here are some of the ways that the series of sentences can be combined:

(a) Agatha Christie, a famous English mystery writer, was missing for 10 days in 1924, and her disappearance made front-page headlines in the British newspapers.

(b) The 10-day disappearance of Agatha Christie, a famous English mystery writer, made front-page headlines in the British newspapers in 1924.

(c) When Agatha Christie dropped out of sight for 10 days in 1924, British newspapers featured the disappearance of the great English mystery writer in front-page headlines.

(d) In 1924, banner headlines in British newspapers announced the 10-day disappearance of the famous English mystery writer, Agatha Christie.

104

(e) Agatha Christie, an Englishwoman who was already famous for her "whodunits," became front-page news in the British press when she disappeared for 10 days in 1924.

Notice that the meaning of each sentence in the original series is preserved in every variation, (a) through (e). In sentence combining, the wording and the order of information can change, but the meaning stays basically the same.

Notes on the Exercises

Some students love sentence combining; others find it monotonous. For most people, the trick is to work on the exercises in chunks of not more than 20 or 30 minutes. If you try to do two or three hours' worth of sentence combining in one sitting, you're probably going to get very little out of the experience. If it starts to seem like busywork, take a break and come back fresh.

Once in a great while, you might find a group of sentences for which you can make only one satisfactory combination. However, for most groups, you'll be able to combine the sentences in a variety of ways. Make at least one combination for each group.

If a numbered "group" actually consists of only one sentence, it's a transitional sentence or a sentence that is short for some other intended effect. This kind of sentence should not be combined with anything else or rephrased.

Sometimes you'll see items that should be put into parallel form. The natural parallelism of some listed items has been altered in order to give you a little challenge here and there.

Exercise 5.1 Odd Moments in the World of Sports

This exercise consists of 10 short items (A-J) based on sports oddities described in *The Great American Sports Book* by George Gipe.

Better Sentence-Writing

A. 1. Two football teams were practicing before a game. The teams were from King's Island, Alaska. They were getting ready for the 1938 New Year's Day Ice Bowl game.
   2. They had been practicing on an ice floe. The ice floe was huge. It was flat. It was near their village.
   3. They went out to practice. The date was December 18, 1937. They couldn't find their practice field. Gale-force winds had blown it away.

B. 1. The French Boxing Federation made a decision. It made the decision in 1924.
   2. The federation issued an official ban. It was a ban against fighters kissing each other. Fighters had traditionally kissed each other at the end of each bout.

C. 1. How slow can you go and still win?
   2. The slowest time for a winning racehorse was set in 1945. It was set during a steeplechase.
   3. The horse was named Never Mind II. Never Mind II refused a jump. His jockey gave up. He returned the horse to the paddock.
   4. When the jockey arrived at the paddock, he learned that all the other horses had met one of two fates. Some of the horses had fallen. The rest had been disqualified.
   5. So he jumped onto Never Mind II. He rode him back onto the track.
   6. Never Mind II won the race. The race was two miles. His winning time was 11 minutes and 28 seconds. The race is normally finished in four minutes.

D. 1. Here's another odd bit of trivia.
It is from the world of horseracing.

   2. A jockey had just won the first race of his career.
His name was Hayes.
The date was June 4, 1923.
After his victory, he immediately dropped dead.

E. 1. The first official baseball game played in the United States took place on June 19, 1846.
It was between the "New York Nine" and the Knickerbockers.

   2. During the game, a New York player swore at the umpire.
He started a baseball tradition by doing so.
The tradition is long.
The tradition is rich.

   3. The New York player was named Davis.
He was fined for his outburst.
The fine was six cents.

F. 1. Hockey is known for its violence.
Most of it seems to be intentional.

   2. But one hockey game was marked by a very unusual incident.
It was an incident of unintentional violence.
It happened in 1930.
The game was in Quebec.
It was a junior amateur game.

   3. A puck was lined at the goalie.
The goalie was Able Goldberry.
The puck struck a pack of matches.
The matches were in Goldberry's pocket.
His uniform caught on fire.

   4. The fire was put out.
It was put out by players and spectators.
Abie Goldberry was badly burned in the bizarre incident.

G. 1. During a basketball game at St. Peter's High School, all of the players on one team, with one exception, fouled out. The game was between sophomores and seniors. The game was played on March 16, 1937. The high school was in Fairmount, Virginia. The exception was Pat McGee.

2. When all the others fouled out, the game was tied.
The score was 32-32.
There were four minutes left to play.

3. It didn't look good for McGee's team.

4. But McGee faced the five players on the opposing team.
He scored a goal. He made a foul shot.
He defended his team's basket.
He prevented his opponents from scoring.

5. McGee won the game for his team.
He did it single-handedly.
The final score was 35-32.

H. 1. In 1958, Robert F. Legge swam the Panama Canal.
Legge was a U.S. Navy doctor.
He was 53 years old.
The canal was 28.5 miles long.
His time was 21 hours and 54 minutes.

2. During the swim, he encountered only two living creatures.
One was a boa constrictor.
The other was an iguana.

3. At times, progress was difficult.
He had to contend with occasional swells.
The swells were a result of the heavy traffic of ships.

4. When he arrived at Balboa, he was met by a greeting party. It consisted of several hundred well-wishers. It also included a toll collector.
The toll collector charged Legge 72 cents.
That was the minimum fee for a one-ton vessel in ballast.

I. 1. In 1890, a postseason baseball series was played.
It was a best-of-seven series.

It was between New York of the National League and St. Louis of the American Association.

2. New York had won three games.
   St. Louis had won two.
   Then the St. Louis Browns won their third game.
   The series was all tied up. It was three games apiece.

3. After they evened up the series, the Browns stayed out all night.
   They were celebrating.
   The next day, they claimed to be "too tuckered out" to take the field.
   As a consequence, the final game was canceled.
   The best-of-seven series still stands as "tied 3-3" in the record books today.

J. 1. In 1865, Louis Fox was playing John Deery in Rochester, New York.
   They were playing pool.
   They were playing for a $1,000 purse.

2. Louis Fox was a billiard champion.
   He was enjoying a very comfortable lead.
   Suddenly, a fly landed on the cue ball.

3. The problem was how to get the fly to move without moving the cue ball.

4. Those who were present tried everything.
   The fly would not budge.
   It didn't matter what anyone did.

5. Fox was more than bugged by the presence of the fly.
   He became completely rattled.

6. He miscued.
   He lost the match with Deery.
   He rushed out of the pool hall.
   He was angry.

7. Several days later, his body was found.
   It was floating in the river.
   The river was near the pool hall.

Many people assumed that Fox committed suicide after his strange loss.

Exercise 5.2 Sweet Dreams

A. 1. Several years ago, the editors of *Psychology Today* asked their readers a question.
   They asked readers if they remembered their dreams.
2. More than 1,000 of the magazine's readers responded.
   Approximately 95 percent of the readers reported that they do remember at least some of their dreams.
   About 68 percent claimed to have a recurring dream.
3. Two different themes were represented most frequently in the recurring dreams.
   One was the experience of being chased.
   The other was the sensation of falling.
4. The readers reported other recurring themes.
   Those themes included flying.
   They included appearing naked or almost naked in a public place.
   Another one was being unprepared to take a test.
   One was the act of returning to the dreamer's childhood home.
5. About 45 percent of the readers said that they sometimes dream about celebrities.
   The celebrities that were noted most frequently were sex symbols and rock stars.
6. After sex symbols and rock stars, people most often reported dreaming about politicians and historical figures.
   One such historical figure was Abraham Lincoln.
7. Lincoln himself put a lot of stock in dreams.
   He believed that one dream had forewarned him of his own assassination.
8. Of those who responded to the *Psychology Today* survey, 28 percent had seen themselves die in a dream.

That sounds very ominous.

Most experts say a dream of one's own death should not be at all frightening.

B. 1. Ann Faraday is a psychologist.

She is the author of *The Dream Game*.

She says that a dream about one's death often indicates something far different from what you might expect.

2. She says it usually symbolizes the death of a self-image. The self-image is obsolete.

She says it signals an opportunity to move to a higher state of self-definition.

3. The interpretation of dreams in general is a highly controversial area.

4. There are those who follow Sigmund Freud.

They believe that dreams are the key to the unconscious.

5. Then there are those who follow the thinking of Francis Crick. He is a Nobel laureate.

He believes that dreams are a garbage disposal for the mind.

6. Their function is to clear out a certain type of information. That information is useless.

It interferes with rational thought.

It interferes with memory.

This is what Crick believes.

7. Then there is a third school of thought.

It consists of psychologists who believe that dreams are not important in themselves.

They believe that dreams become important because people think they are important.

8. These psychologists believe that people give dreams meaning.

People give them influence.

They give them power.

Exercise 5.3 A Giant of a Man

A. 1. *The People's Almanac #3* includes a cautionary tale.
The almanac is the work of David Wallechinsky and Irving Wallace.
The tale is for anyone who has ever daydreamed about what it would be like to be a giant.
2. It is not a tall tale.
It is a true story.
It is the story of Robert Wadlow.
He was probably the tallest person who has ever lived.
3. Wadlow was born in Alton, Illinois.
He was born on February 22, 1918.
His weight at birth was nothing unusual.
He was eight-and-a-half pounds.
4. His family's medical history was normal.
There were no unusually tall members in his family.
5. But he grew rapidly.
He grew steadily.
This was true from birth.
It didn't stop until his death.
6. He was weighed at six months.
He was 30 pounds.
The average six-month-old baby weighs from 15 to 17 pounds.
7. He was weighed again at 18 months. His weight was 62 pounds.
The average toddler at that age weighs 24 or 25 pounds.
8. He underwent his first thorough examination at the age of 5. He was five feet, four inches tall. He weighed 105 pounds.
9. He started school when he was five and a half.
He was wearing clothes made for 17-year-olds.

10. He was measured again at the age of 8. He had reached a height of six feet. His father was Robert Wadlow, Sr. His father started wearing hand-me-downs. The hand-me-downs came from his son.

B. 1. When Robert Wadlow was 12, his rapid growth was finally diagnosed.
The diagnosis was excessive pituitary gland secretion.
After that, careful records of his growth were kept.
They were kept at Washington University.
Washington University is in St. Louis, Missouri.

2. He grew an average of three inches a year.
This rate of growth continued throughout his entire life.
At his death, his height was eight feet, eleven inches.
He died on July 15, 1940.

3. His early death was not surprising.

4. Pituitary giants usually die before middle age.
Their organs outgrow the ability to function correctly.

5. Physical coordination becomes difficult for a giant.
As a result, a giant usually has many more accidents than a normal-sized person has.

6. A giant's accidents also tend to result in more serious injuries.
This problem is compounded by the fact that a giant's body heals more slowly.

7. Wadlow in particular had more than his share of physical problems.
They began with an operation for a double hernia.
The operation took place when he was 2 years old.

8. Everything he encountered in this world was on the wrong scale.
School desks were too small.
Doorways were too low.
Beds were too short.
Chairs were too tiny.

9. He had terrible problems with his feet.

10. Doctors advised Wadlow to walk as much as possible.
Walking was supposed to build up the strength in his feet.
It did not.
It damaged his arches even more severely.
11. For a while, he attended Shurtleff College.
He wanted to become a lawyer.
He had to drop out.
The reason was that it was too difficult for him to walk from classroom to classroom.

C. 1. Robert Wadlow's life was marked by tragedy.
His life was not completely tragic.
2. He was intelligent.
He was charming.
He had good parents.
They tried to make his life as normal as possible.
They tried to make it as full as possible.
3. His boyhood days were filled with typical things.
They were filled with hobbies.
They were filled with sports.
He belonged to the Boy Scouts.
He loved to read.
4. But his life was also filled with things that were not so typical.
5. The more unusual aspects of Wadlow's story started when he was discovered by the media.
That discovery happened when he was 9 years old.
6. It happened when the Associated Press came across a photograph.
The Associated Press circulated it in newspapers all across the nation.
7. That's when Robert Wadlow became a public person.
8. From that time on, he had to deal with a steady stream of people.
Some were reporters.

Some were medical researchers.
Some were curiosity seekers.
Some were entrepreneurs.
9. Theatrical agents pressured him to perform.
They made very attractive offers.
They wanted his services.
10. His parents rejected all opportunities to make money from his misfortune.
11. He did, however, make appearances for the Peters Shoe Company.
They were paid appearances.
The Peters Shoe Company was in St. Louis.
12. This endorsement arrangement was appropriate.
Wadlow had to have specially made shoes.
He often outgrew new shoes even before they were delivered.
13. Robert Wadlow also worked for the Ringling Brothers Circus.
He worked for Ringling Brothers in New York and Boston.
He did so for a short time.
This was in 1937.
There were strict conditions in his contract with the circus.
14. These were the conditions of the contract.
He would make only three-minute appearances.
He would make them in the center ring.
He would not make them in the sideshow.
He would wear ordinary street clothes for these appearances.
15. Wadlow occasionally made appearances for churches.
He also helped to raise funds for charities.
He accepted no pay for these activities.
D. 1. In 1936, Robert Wadlow had a visit from a doctor.
He was a doctor from a small town in Missouri.

The doctor was interested in studying giantism.
2. He happened to catch Wadlow on a bad day.
   Bad days were relatively rare for Wadlow.
3. The doctor later wrote an article about Wadlow.
   The article was published in the *Journal of the American Medical Association.*
   The article described Wadlow as dull.
   It described him as surly.
4. According to information cited in *The People's Almanac #3,* this characterization is generally true of most pathological giants.
   It was not true of Robert Wadlow.
   He was truly an exceptional human being.
5. The unflattering description in the medical journal hurt Wadlow deeply.
   It disillusioned him.
   It did so for two reasons.
6. For one thing, all his life he had put up with medical researchers.
   The medical researchers had invaded his privacy.
   They had taken up his time.
   He always had done so voluntarily.
   He usually had done so graciously.
7. For another thing, the article was based on the doctor's impressions.
   Those impressions were made very quickly.
   The doctor's only visit with Wadlow had lasted less than an hour.
8. Wadlow wanted his character vindicated.
   His family did, too.
   They took legal action against the doctor.
   They also took legal action against the American Medical Association (AMA).
9. The AMA strongly defended the doctor.
   The litigation dragged on and on.

116

The matter was not resolved when Wadlow died.
He died at the age of 22.

10. Robert Wadlow stipulated that after his death he wanted his body to be kept out of the hands of medical researchers.
His stipulation was partly the result of this episode.

11. In accordance with his wishes, there was no examination of his body after his death.

12. He was buried in a custom-built casket.
The casket was 10 feet long.
The casket was placed inside a tomb.
The tomb was almost impregnable.
The tomb was in his hometown.

13. More than 46,000 people came to the funeral home in Alton, Illinois.
They paid their last respects to Robert Wadlow.

Exercise 5.4 Control and Well-being

A. 1. Judith Rodin is a psychology professor.
She teaches at Yale University.
She has been involved in important studies on a number of topics.
One topic is bystander intervention.
One is learned helplessness.
One is obesity.
One is aging.

2. She is interested in relationships.
One that especially interests her is the relationship between the mind and the body.
Another one is the relationship between biology and environment.

3. Older people, in particular, have benefitted from Rodin's research.

4. In fact, it's been said that it's not easy for her to find places in Connecticut where she can continue to study the problems of older people in nursing homes.
   This is because so many positive changes already have been made in the state's nursing homes as a result of her work.
5. Rodin conducted a study on perceived choice among residents of nursing homes.
   She did this at one point in her career.
   She did this with psychologist Ellen Langer. The study was fascinating.
   It was described in an issue of *Psychology Today*.
6. Perceived choice is the amount of control that a person believes he or she has over events.
7. Rodin already knew that the degree to which people feel they can exert control in important areas of their lives influences three things.
   It influences their happiness.
   It influences their ability to perform.
   It influences their sense of well-being.
   She knew this on the basis of laboratory studies.
B. 1. Judith Rodin and Ellen Langer wanted to investigate perceived choice or control in a real-life setting.
   The real-life setting they chose was a nursing home.
2. They were especially interested in one relationship.
   It was the relationship between the degree of control that the nursing home residents thought they had and the residents' health and happiness.
3. Rodin and Langer believed that a nursing home might be a place where the effects of increased control could show up dramatically.
   Improvements in well-being could be quite obvious.
   They would show up in people who were already sick or frail.

4. It would be more difficult to show the positive benefits of an increased sense of control in people who were younger and healthier.
   In those people, any benefits would more likely be in the form of prevention rather than improvement.
5. The results of the study were indeed dramatic.
6. Nursing home residents in the study were given new choices. These were in areas in which they previously had no choice.
   Many of the new choices seemed quite trivial.
7. For example, residents were allowed to choose when they could see a movie.
   They were allowed to arrange their rooms as they wished.
C. 1. The choices may have been trivial.
   The results were not.
2. The researchers used a variety of methods to measure the effects of the residents' new sense of control.
   The researchers discovered that the residents' new sense of control had a number of effects.
   One effect was an improvement in their health.
   One effect was an improvement in their overall mental state.
   One effect was a drop in the death rate at the nursing home.
3. Why would having new choices in trivial areas of life produce such profound effects?
4. Rodin explains that the choices seem trivial only to people who have a broad range of choices in their lives.
   To those who have little or no choice, any choice at all has great impact.
5. A sense of control or perceived choice created a profound psychological state.
   It is a state in which the residents felt better about themselves.
6. They felt a sense of power.

That sense of power caused them to respond more positively to family members.

It caused them to respond more positively to other residents.

It caused them to respond more positively to nurses and doctors.

In turn, everyone in their lives responded more positively toward them.

7. Choosing when to see a movie or where to put a picture on a wall might seem trivial.

But Rodin says that small bit of control can have an energizing effect. It can have that effect on every aspect of an older person's life.

Exercise 5.5 Mabel K. Staupers and Black Nurses in the Military

A. 1. Mabel Keaton Staupers was one of the outstanding women of the twentieth century.

She was a black woman.

She was fast-talking.

She was energetic.

2. She broke a link in a chain.

She did it almost single-handedly.

It was a chain that had kept many black women from using their talents and skills.

It was a chain that had denied them their full rights as American citizens.

3. Her story is fascinating.

It is inspiring.

It is a classic David and Goliath tale.

It is told in *Black Leaders of the Twentieth Century*.

4. It is the story of a battle between one woman and two branches of the American military.

The woman was the executive secretary of the National Association of Colored Graduate Nurses (NACGN).

The branches of the military were the U.S. Army and the Navy.

5. Mabel K. Staupers's accomplishment must be viewed within the context of a certain period in American history if it is to be fully appreciated.

6. It was around the time that the United States entered into World War II.
   American blacks recently had become much less accepting of the racial status quo.
   There were many reasons for this.
   One was the anti-Nazi mood of the nation.

7. For many blacks, their unequal treatment in their own country was highlighted in an ironic way by America's opposition to Nazi Germany.

8. In opposing the philosophy and actions of Germany's Nazis, the U.S. government did a lot of talking.
   So did many members of the press.
   So did much of the general public.
   They all talked a lot about the ideals upon which America had been founded.

9. They contrasted Germany to an America that was pure in the realization of its democratic ideals.
   They spoke of an America that was just in its treatment of people of different backgrounds.
   The differences might be in religion, ethnicity, or race.

10. Such statements about this country struck some Americans as hypocritical.
    They struck some Americans as ironic.
    Some of those Americans were black.
    Some were white.

11. One person summed this up the situation well.
    He was Walter White.
    He wrote, "World War II has immeasurably magnified the Negro's awareness of the disparity between the American profession and practice of democracy."

Better Sentence-Writing

B. 1. It was during this time and in this context that Mabel K. Staupers began her long fight.
   Her fight was for the rights of black nurses.
   She used patience.
   She used persistence.
   She used a great deal of political savvy.
2. Staupers was born in Barbados, West Indies.
   She was born in 1890.
   She came to New York with her parents.
   They came to New York in 1903.
3. She graduated from Freedmen's Hospital School of Nursing.
   It was in Washington, D.C.
   She graduated in 1917.
   Then she began her career.
   Her first position was as a private nurse in New York City.
4. She played an important role in establishing the Booker T. Washington Sanatorium.
   The Booker T. Washington Sanatorium was in Harlem.
   It was the first facility in the area where black doctors could treat patients.
5. Then she worked as the executive secretary for the Harlem Committee of the New York Tuberculosis and Health Association.
   She did that for 12 years.
6. Finally, Staupers was appointed executive secretary of the NACGN.
   That was in 1934.
   In her new position, she focused on one main goal.
   That goal was to help black nurses become fully integrated into the mainstream of American health care.
7. Then the United States entered World War II.
   It was 1941.
8. Mabel K. Staupers had a perfect opportunity to realize her goal.

The war created a great demand for nurses to care for the wounded.

9. That demand could result in the acceptance of black nurses into the Army and Navy Nurse Corps.
   That acceptance could be a vehicle.
   It could be a vehicle for the full inclusion of blacks into the profession of nursing in America.

C. 1. Staupers knew that black nurses had suffered great discrimination in World War I.
   She vowed that would not happen again if she could help it.

2. So Staupers fought her own battle.
   She fought it throughout the years of the American war effort.
   She fought it on various fronts.

3. First, she fought the exclusion of black women from the Army and Navy Nurse Corps.

4. Then the Army established a quota system for black nurses.
   She fought the quota system.
   She fought it because it implied that black nurses were inferior to other nurses.

5. At one point, she fought another policy of the military.
   It was the policy of having black nurses care for black soldiers and no others.

6. Later, she discovered the Army was finally assigning black nurses to care for white soldiers.
   But those white soldiers included no Americans.
   The white soldiers were German prisoners of war.
   She fought that practice, too.

D. 1. These were tough battles.
   Staupers eventually found a powerful ally.
   That ally was First Lady Eleanor Roosevelt.

2. Eleanor Roosevelt began lobbying for black nurses.

3. She talked to Norman T. Kirk.
   He was the surgeon general of the U.S. Army.

She talked to W.J.C. Agnew.

He was a rear admiral in the U.S. Navy.

Most of all, she talked to her husband.

Her husband was Franklin D. Roosevelt.

4. Meanwhile, Staupers staged a public confrontation with Norman T. Kirk.

It was a confrontation that received a good deal of coverage in the press.

5. Kirk described the dire shortage of nurses in the Army.

He predicted that a draft for nurses might be necessary.

He made his prediction in a speech at the Hotel Pierre.

The Hotel Pierre is in New York.

6. Staupers was in Kirk's audience.

The audience was made up of about 300 people.

The audience included nurses.

It included politicians.

It included private citizens.

7. She rose to her feet.

She asked the surgeon general, "If nurses are needed so desperately, why isn't the Army using colored nurses?"

8. She explained to the entire audience that there were 9,000 registered black nurses in the United States.

The Army had taken 247.

The Navy had taken none.

9. Kirk was visibly uncomfortable, according to newspaper reports.

He did not have much of an answer for Staupers.

E. 1. At about the same time, President Roosevelt announced his desire to amend the Selective Service Act of 1940.

He wanted it amended so that nurses could be drafted.

He made his desire known in a radio address.

The address was broadcast on January 6, 1945.

2. The public reaction was tremendous.

The irony of calling for a general draft while at the same time discriminating against black nurses was obvious to almost everyone.

3. Staupers showed a lot of political savvy in the way she handled the public's dissatisfaction with the plans of the top brass.
4. She gave speeches.
   She issued press releases.
   She urged people to send telegrams to President Roosevelt.
5. The groups that sent messages of protest to the White House included the National Association for the Advancement of Colored People (NAACP).
   They included the Congress of Industrial Organizations.
   They included the American Federation of Labor.
   They included the United Council of Church Women.
   They included the Catholic Interracial Council.
   They included the Alpha Kappa Alpha Sorority.
   They included the New York Citizens' Committee of the Upper West Side.
6. The great wave of public protest had an effect.
   The policies of exclusion, segregation, and quota systems for black nurses were ended.
   They were dropped by the Army.
   They were dropped by the Navy.
   They were dropped by the War Department.
7. A few weeks later, a black woman was the first to break the color barrier in the U.S. Navy Nurse Corps.
   She was Phyllis Dailey.
8. The Army also began to accept black nurses with no restrictions.
9. Most of the credit goes to one woman.
   It goes to one woman alone.
   It goes to Mabel K. Staupers.

Chapter 6

Revising at the Word Level

6.1 Subject-Verb Agreement

We all follow a system of subject-verb agreement, even if we can't define what subject-verb agreement is. If you listen to your speech and the speech of your family and friends, you'll find that most people follow a fairly consistent pattern. For instance, you probably say *she smiles* and *he laughs*. In other words, you have your own unconscious rules about adding *-s* or *-es* on a verb when it's in the present tense. But if your system differs from the one that is considered standard, you may want to make an adjustment in your writing.

The Standard Rules

Basically, subject-verb agreement is a problem only in the present tense. Here are the standard rules:

1. If the Subject Is Singular, Add -S or -Es to Your Verb

For example:

                        s   v

(a) One teenage *suicide occurs* every 90 minutes in the United States.

127

The subject *suicide* is singular (one), so we added an *-s* to the verb *occur* and produced *occurs*. Now we'll make the subject plural (more than one) and see how the verb changes to agree with it:

            s   v

(b) Teenage *suicides* occur at the rate of one every ninety minutes in the United States.

The rule shown in (b) is this:

2. If the Subject Is Plural, Use the Base Verb

The word *suicides* is plural, so we used the base verb occur to agree with it. By *base verb* we mean a verb with no ending B no *-s* or *-es,* no *-d* or *-ed*, no *-ing* or any other ending.

Label the subject in each example below and fill in the standard form of the verb, choosing from *live* and *lives:*

1. The pint-sized sand cat _____ on the extremely hot sand dunes of African, Asian, and Arabian deserts.

2. Pint-sized sand cats _____ on the extremely hot sand dunes of African, Asian, and Arabian deserts.

If you used an *-s* in sentence 1 and the base verb in sentence 2, you're on the right track.

Study these correct examples and read them aloud several times before you do the first exercise:

(a) a steak sizzles	(d) the roof leaks	(f) a balloon pops
steaks sizzle	roofs often leak	balloons pop
(b) the horse prances	(e) the girl stretches	(g) the group decides
horses prance	the girls stretch	the groups decide
(c) one light flickers		
five lights flicker		

Exercise 6.1

Fill in each blank with the form of verb at right that agrees with the subject. Use the base verb or add *-s* or *-es*. For example:

the plan   succeeds   (succeed)
the plans   succeed

1. a carpenter _____ (build)
   carpenters _____

2. one star _____ (shine)
   all the stars _____

3. the golfer _____ (putt)
   golfers _____

4. roses _____ (grow)
   a rose _____

5. the chimneys _____ (smoke)
   the chimney _____

6. a pitcher _____ (pitch)
   pitchers _____

7. one loaf _____ (rise)
   the loaves _____

8. bombs _____ (explode)
   a bomb _____

9. the popside _____ (melt)
   popsicles _____

10. last-minute shoppers _____ (rush)
    a last-minute shopper _____

A Note on Spelling

In the next exercise, you'll notice that sometimes a small spelling change is necessary before you add an *-s* or *-es* to a base verb. For example, with a word that ends in -y, such as *fry,* you change the y to i before you add -es. So *fry* becomes *fries.*

Exercise 6.2

Fill in each blank with the form of verb at right that agrees with the subject. Use the base verb or add -s or -es. Make other spelling changes where necessary.

1. the article _____ (explain)
   the articles _____

2. one baby _____ (cry)
   all the babies _____

3. one player _____ (win)
   four players _____

4. the team _____ (perform)
   the teams _____

5. the ink spots _____ (dry)
   an ink spot _____

6. the soldiers _____ (march)
   a soldier _____

7. the telephone _____ (ring)
   telephones _____

8. ideas _____ (form)
   an idea _____

9. chickens _____ (hatch)
   a chicken _____

10. a peacemaker _____ (pacify)
    peacemakers _____

Two Important Exceptions

There are two important exceptions to the standard rules described here. One involves the word *I*, and the other involves the word *you*. When *I* and *you* are used as subjects, they always appear with the base verb. These are correct examples: *I want, I sing,* and *I give; you want, you sing,* and *you give.* Even though *I* is singular and *you* can be singular or plural in its meaning, each pronoun—*I* and *you*—agrees with a base verb.

The Verbs *To Be* and *To Have*

Here's an easy way to approach subject-verb agreement when the verb is a form of *to be* or *to have*. Just as with regular verbs, the correct form to match a singular subject will end in -*s*. The correct form to match a plural subject will not end in -*s*. Study these correct examples:

Singular Subject	Plural Subject
The dessert *is* delicious.	The desserts *are* delicious.
The dessert *was* delicious.	The desserts *were* delicious.
The dessert *has* pizzazz.	The desserts *have* pizzazz.

Notice that all the words that agree with the singular subject *dessert* end in -*s: is, was,* and *has.* Also notice that the verbs that agree with the plural subject *desserts* do not end in -*s*. They are *are, were,* and *have.*

Exercise 6.3

Fill in each blank with the verb that agrees with the subject. Remember: A singular subject agrees with a verb that ends in -*s*—with the exceptions of *I* and *you*, which are treated as plural subjects.

1. A Steven Spielberg movie _____ *(has / have)* certain characteristics.

Better Sentence-Writing

Steven Spielberg movies _____ *(has / have)* certain characteristics.

2. Her attitude _____ *(is / are)* wonderful.
   Their attitudes _____ *(is / are)* wonderful.

3. The mail carriers _____ *(was / were)* late.
   The mail carrier _____ *(was / were)* late.

4. Soft pretzels _____ *(is / are)* one of life's little necessities.
   A soft pretzel _____ *(is / are)* one of life's little necessities.

5. One fingernail _____ *(was / were)* polished with jade green lacquer.
   Her fingernails _____ *(was / were)* polished with jade green lacquer.

Three Important Points

There are three important points about subject-verb agreement that everyone should know. We'll look at each one before you begin the more difficult exercises.

1. Using And and Or between Key Words in the Subject

You probably already know that two singular words joined with and form a plural subject. But you should also know that two singular words joined with or form a singular subject. Study these correct examples:

(a) A magazine <u>subscription</u> **and** a book club <u>membership</u> <u>make</u> good gifts for the person who has everything.

(b) A magazine <u>subscription</u> **or** a book club <u>membership</u> <u>makes</u> a good gift for the person who has everything.

132

2. Using Prepositional Phrases in the Subject

Remember when you worked with prepositional phrases in Chapter 1? The key word in the subject is never within a prepositional phrase, and the key word in the subject is, of course, the word with which the verb must agree. So you have to be careful to set off any prepositional phrases that appear within the complete subject of a sentence.

Study these correct examples:

           s   v

(a) Rock and roll <u>festivals</u> <u>are</u> a common feature of summertime entertainment.

        s   v

(b) Any <u>history</u> (of rock and roll festivals) <u>is</u> sure to begin with the concert at Woodstock.

In (a), the word *festivals* is the key word in the subject, and because it is plural, it agrees with *are*. But in (b), the word *festivals* is not the key word in thesubject. Why not? It's not the key word because it's in a prepositional phrase—*of rock and roll festivals.* (The preposition is *of.*) A prepositional phrase modifies the subject, but it never contains the subject.

In (b), the key word in the subject is *history,* and because *history* is a singular word, it agrees with the verb *is.*

3. Using Delayed Subjects

There are two kinds of sentences that have delayed subjects. A subject is called "delayed" when it follows the verb.

One kind of sentence with a delayed subject begins with the word *there* or *here.* If a sentence begins with either word, you have to look beyond the verb to find the real subject—the word with which the verb must agree. Study these correct examples:

        v   s

1. (a) There <u>was</u> one bad <u>joke</u> in the middle of the script.

        v   s

(b) There <u>were</u> several bad <u>jokes</u> in the middle of the script.

        v   s

2. (a) Here <u>is</u> the best <u>play</u> of the day.

        v   s

(b) Here <u>are</u> the two best <u>plays</u> of the day.

Think of the words *there* and *here* as empty sentence starters. They're not the subjects in any of the preceding four sentences. They're sort of placeholders that indicate where the subject word would normally be.

The other kind of sentence with a delayed subject is a question. In the following sentences, the question word acts in the same way as *there* or *here*. Study these correct examples:

        v   s

3. (a) What <u>is</u> your <u>plan</u>?

        v   s

(b) What <u>are</u> your <u>plans</u>?

        v   s

4. (a) Where <u>was</u> his new <u>shirt</u>?

        v   s

(b) Where <u>were</u> his new <u>shirts</u>?

Important Note on the Exercises

The next two exercises involve all the points covered in this unit. If you need to review, please do so before you proceed.

In the exercises, when the directions ask you to label the subject, please understand that you're really being asked to mark the *key word or words* within the complete subject.

Exercise 6.4

Write *s* over the subject of each clause. Then fill in the blank with the form of the verb that agrees with the subject.

1. According to the latest records kept by the U.S. Agriculture Department, 1,431 pounds of food _____ *(are/is)* consumed by the average American in one year. Twenty years ago, the average intake of food per person _____ *(was/were)* 1,381 pounds. Forecasters in the department's Economic Research Service *(say/says)* that increases in the consumption of chicken, fish, vegetables, and vegetable oil _____ *(are/is)* expected. Meat and fruit _____ *(appear/appears)* to be on the decline.

2. The correct term for American buffaloes _____ *(are/is)* American bison.

3. Only the true fan among fans _____ *(care/cares)* enough about sports trivia to know that the real names of "the Georgia Peach" and "the Galloping Ghost" _____ *(was/were)* Ty Cobb and Red Grange.

4. According to chiropractors, poor posture habits in a child usually _____ *(begin/begins)* around age eight.

5. *Final Payments* and *The Company of Women* _____ *(are/is)* excellent novels by Mary Gordon. *Men and Angels* _____ *(are/is)* another of her books.

Better Sentence-Writing

Exercise 6.5

Write *s* over the subject of each clause. Then fill in the blank with the verb that agrees with the subject. This collection of strange facts *(are / is)* based on information in *Life-spans, Or, How Long Things Last.*

1. One of every seven pennies in circulation eventually _____ *(end / ends)* up out of circulation. This _____ *(happen / happens)* because the penny's owner _____ *(plunk / plunks)* it into a piggy bank or _____ *(force / forces)* it into early retirement in the bottom of a dresser drawer or in an inner compartment of an old purse. One of every 14 nickels _____ *(share / shares)* a similar fate.

2. Most nuts _____ *(stay / stays)* fresh for one year if they _____ *(remain / remains)* in the shell. However, pecans and Brazil nuts _____ *(keep / keeps)* for only six months unless you _____ *(store / stores)* them in the refrigerator.

3. Moonbeams, which _____ *(are / is)* rays of light from the sun reflected off the moon, _____ *(take / takes)* 1.3 seconds to travel from the moon to the earth.

4. The life span of a deck of cards _____ *(depend / depends)* upon a number of factors. The moisture in the hands of the card players _____ *(are / is)* one important factor because the moisture and oil in human skin definitely _____ *(affect / affects)* the cards' longevity. The condition of any and all playing surfaces on which the cards (are/is) used _____ *(are / is)* also significant. For some people a deck of cards _____ *(last / lasts)* a lifetime. For professional gamblers, the average pack _____ *(has / have)* outgrown its usefulness

after two to five hours of playing time. After that, the cards usually _____ *(show / shows)* enough wear and tear that they _____ *(slow / slows)* down the dealer if they _____ *(are / is)* not replaced with a fresh pack.

5. A series of elastic waves, most often caused by the earth's rupture along a fault, _____ *(are / is)* better known as an earthquake. The length of most earthquakes _____ *(are / is)* not more than a few seconds, but major earthquakes, such as the one in Lisbon, Portugal, in 1975, _____ *(has / have)* been clocked at over five minutes. Certainly one of the most devastating earthquakes in recent times _____ *(was / were)* the one to hit Mexico City in September 1985.

6.2 *-Ed* Endings

The purpose of this unit is to help students who sometimes drop the *-d* or *-ed* endings on regular verbs and the adjectives made from them.

First you need to be able to distinguish between *regular* and *irregular* verbs. If a verb is regular, its past tense and past participle are formed by adding *-d* or *-ed* to the base verb. For example:

Base Verb	Past Tense	Past Participle
ask	asked	have asked

If a verb is irregular (in other words, not regular), it does not follow this nice, easy pattern of adding *-d* or *-ed*. For example, *give* is an irregular verb. Here are its three main forms:

Base Verb	Past Tense	Past Participle
give	gave	have given

You're already familiar with base verbs and past tenses, but the term *past participle* might be new to you. What does it mean? The *past participle* is the form of a verb that is used with helping verbs such as *have, has,* or a form of the verb *to be* when it is used to make the passive voice. (See Chapter 4 if you need to review the definition of *passive voice*). These examples show how the presence of a helping verb signals the need for a *-d* to be added to the regular verb purchase:

(a) *I have purchased* the suit.

(b) She *has purchased* the apartment building.

(c) He *had purchased* the license only thirty minutes before the wedding.

(d) The tainted medicine *was purchased* in a drug store two miles from the victim's home.

(e) Fourteen square acres in the middle of the city *were purchased* by an international corporation.

The Three Trouble Spots

When writers drop *-d* and *-ed* endings, they drop them on *past tense verbs, past participles,* and *adjectives that are derived from verbs.* Of these three trouble spots, the first—past tense—is the easiest to catch. The other two are more challenging. Study these correct examples:

(a) Yesterday the doctor *prescribed* a basic blood pressure medicine for Carl. (past tense)

(b) Another specialist *has prescribed* treatment for him on several occasions. (past participle)

(c) The *prescribed* pills were very effective. (adjective derived from a verb)

You can probably see why most students would have the least difficulty with (a). The word *Yesterday* is a context clue for the past tense, and that helps the writer remember to add the *-d* to *prescribe*.

In (b) and (c), there are no obvious context clues for the past tense, but there are other clues for the student who's wondering whether to use a *-d*. The clue in (b) is the helping verb *has*. And sometimes, as you'll see in the exercises, a sentence contains more than one helping verb. For example, you'll see sentences with longer verb phrases, such as this one:

A third doctor *might have prescribed* something else.

In (c) the clue is the noun *pills*. Someone did the act of prescribing the pills, and now they can be described as *prescribed*. Adjectives that are made from regular verbs end in *-d* or *-ed*.

In this set of three examples, add *-d* where it belongs and, each time, make a note of why you added it:

1. Sharon had change tremendously since high school.

2. After the birth of his first child, Gregory was a change man.

3. We change our phone number after a few crank calls.

1. verb phrase; 2. adjective; 3. past tense

Two Notes on Spelling

There are two spelling rules that you need to remember.

1. With a verb that ends in *y*, you usually change the *y* to *i* before you add *-ed*. For example: fry → fried; satisfy → satisfied

2. With a verb that ends in a consonant preceded by a short vowel, you usually double the consonant before you add *-ed*. For example: trip → tripped; wrap → wrapped

Better Sentence-Writing

Some Common Errors

There are a few common errors that many students make. They involve *used to, supposed to, old-fashioned,* and *prejudiced.* Add *-d* or *-ed* where they are needed in these sentences:

1. I use to be afraid of the dark.
2. Jane is really an old-fashion girl.
3. We are suppose to be home by midnight.
4. That was a prejudice remark if I ever heard one.
5. Do you suppose we can get some ice cream?
6. Prejudice is the act of prejudging.
7. The thing that use to drive me crazy was his gum chewing.
8. They were suppose to preregister to vote.
9. I do not believe that this is a prejudice community.

1. used; 2. old-fashioned; 3. supposed; 4. prejudiced; 5. no change; 6. no change; 7. used; 8. supposed; 9. prejudiced.

Exercise 6.6

Add *-d* or *-ed* endings where they are needed. Underline the word that you change and in the blank provided label your reason for the change. Use the labels *past* for past tense verb, *vp* for verb phrase, and *adj* for an adjective derived from a verb.

1. Charlotte Corday murder Jean Paul Marat, a famous eighteenth-century French revolutionary, while he was taking a bath. _____

2. Shredded wheat, the world's first ready-to-eat dry cereal, was introduce in 1893. _____

3. In 1956, a trailer truck that was hauling four hundred crates of eggs slammed into the Rhyne Bridge in Charlotte, North Carolina. The bill for the damage truck and bridge came to six thousand dollars. But guess what? Not one egg was broken. _____

4. *The Fire Next Time* by James Baldwin is a distinguish collection of essays on the hearts and minds of African-Americans. _____

5. In his paintings, Monet capture the colors of the water lilies and other flowers in his famous ponds and gardens at Giverny, France. _____

6. The much admire *Huckleberry Finn* by Mark Twain is often called the greatest novel of American boyhood. _____

7. The first zoo in the history of the world was establish in Egypt around 1500 B.C. _____

8. According to a recent study of hundreds of couples, morning sickness and other pregnancy-related symptoms are experience by one in ten expectant fathers.

9. Yes, the last word in sentence 8 is suppose to be *fathers,* not *mothers.* _____

10. The same study show that one in ten new fathers also suffered from postpartum blues. _____

The Irregular Verbs

The irregular verbs are not as easy to form as those that end in *-d* or *-ed*. To learn these, you have to memorize them. Here is a list of the most frequently used irregular verbs. Underline the verb forms that sound unfamiliar to you; then practice them in your writing as often as you can. We're using *have* as the helping verb here, but you know that other helping verbs are used as well.

141

Better Sentence-Writing

Present	Past	Past Participle
become	became	have become
begin	began	have begun
break	broke	have broken
bring	brought	have brought
buy	bought	have bought
build	built	have built
choose	chose	have chosen
come	came	have come
do	did	have done
drive	drove	have driven
eat	ate	have eaten
fall	fell	have fallen
feel	felt	have felt
fight	fought	have fought
find	found	have found
forget	forgot	have forgotten
forgive	forgave	have forgiven
get	got	have gotten
give	gave	have given
go	went	have gone
grow	grew	have grown
keep	kept	have kept
know	knew	have known
lead	led	have led
leave	left	have left
lose	lost	have lost
make	made	have made
meet	met	have met
pay	paid	have paid

Present	Past	Past Participle
read	read	have read
ride	rode	have ridden
rise	rose	have risen
run	ran	have run
say	said	have said
see	saw	have seen
sell	sold	have sold
sing	sang	have sung
sleep	slept	have slept
speak	spoke	have spoken
spend	spent	have spent
stand	stood	have stood
take	took	have taken
teach	taught	have taught
tell	told	have told
think	thought	have thought
throw	threw	have thrown
wear	wore	have worn
win	won	have won
write	wrote	have written

6.3 Consistency of Verb Tense

What's wrong with this sentence?

I was driving to work, and my car runs out of gas.

The problem is that the writer started the sentence in the past tense (with *was driving*) and ended it in the present tense (with *runs*). If there is a logical reason for switching into another verb

143

tense, it's fine to do so. But what logical reason could this writer have? The sentence has two possible corrections:

Past tense: I <u>was driving</u> to work, and my car <u>ran</u> out of gas.

Present tense: I <u>am driving</u> to work, and my car <u>runs</u> out of gas.

Correct illogical changes in verb tense in these examples:

1. Archduke Franz Ferdinand of Austria was killed in Sarajevo in June 1914, and his assassination sets off World War I.
2. Marcus Garvey, who was the most influential black leader in the United States in the 1920s, advocates black separatism and leads a "back to Africa" movement.
3. Mars is the fourth planet in order of distance from the sun, and to the naked eye, it appeared to have a reddish tint.

In 1, *sets off* should be *set off;* in 2, *advocates should be* advocated, and *leads* should be *led;* and in 3, *appeared* should be *appears.*

Logical Changes in Verb Tense

What's a good reason for switching verb tenses? Maybe you want to write about something that used to be true and no longer is. For example, you might write, "When I *was* a child, I *wanted* to watch cartoons bright and early every Saturday morning, but now, I *like* to sleep until noon." The first clause describes something that was true in the past, so it's natural to use the past tense; the second clause describes something that is true in the present, so it's natural to use the present tense. This is not an example of illogical tense switching. The sentence would lack logic if the writer *didn't* switch tenses.

But switching verb tenses without a good reason causes a lot of trouble for many students. In fact, if tenses are switched back and forth just a few times, a student's paper can look much less organized than it really is. Any piece of writing that has illogical or inconsistent verb tenses seems incoherent; the writer appears to lack control of his or her material.

Writing About Literature

Sometimes it's natural to write a paper predominantly in the past tense, and sometimes it's natural to write mostly in the present tense. Occasionally, you have a choice. For example, a writer can often talk about literature in either the past or the present tense. The reason for this is that although a piece of literature was written in the past we tend to think of it as something that lives in the present. Therefore, in writing about *The Great Gatsby* by F. Scott Fitzgerald, we can choose to say, "Jay Gatsby *represented* the American dream" or "Jay Gatsby *represents* the American dream." The important thing is to be consistent. If you choose to write about a work of literature in the present tense, stay with the present tense; if you choose to use the past, stay with the past.

The Helping Verb *Had*

The helping verb *had* is used when you are writing in the past tense and you wish to indicate something that happened even earlier. For instance, these are correct examples:

(a) Samantha *started* breakfast at seven o'clock this morning; by that time, she *had read* the morning paper and *washed* two loads of clothes.

(b) Frank *had visited* France three times in the 1970s and 1980s before he *made* his first trip with Catherine last year.

Better Sentence-Writing

A Note about *Will/Would* and *Can/Could*

Before beginning the exercises for this unit, it's important for you to realize that the verb *would* is the past tense of *will,* and the verb *could* is the past tense of *can.* For example:

1. (a) He *will* bake a chocolate pecan pie today.
   (b) He *would* have baked a chocolate pecan pie yesterday if he had found the ingredients he needed.
2. (a) Right now I *can* hardly wait for my children to get home.
   (b) Yesterday I *could* hardly wait for my children to get home.

Many students have trouble with the helping verb *would.* It's a mistake to use it when you really mean the simple past tense. For example, it's an error to write, "When I lived in New York, I *would see* at least two plays a week." Why is this wrong? It's wrong because the writer simply means that he or she *saw* at least two plays a week.

The word *would* should be used only when the writer means that something would happen only if a certain condition were fulfilled. The condition is usually found in a clause that begins with the word *if,* but the condition can also be implied rather than stated. Notice in 1 (b) that the writer *would* have baked the pie only *if he had found the ingredients he needed.* First he had to have the ingredients — that's the condition that had to be fulfilled before he would bake the pie.

If you're writing about something that happened often in the past but there's no condition to be fulfilled, no notion of "if" involved, simply use the past tense. Don't add *would.* To check your understanding, mark each sentence below *correct or incorrect:*

1. Marty would have been on time if he had been given the right directions. _____

2. Aunt Dana would kiss you if you stood still for a minute. _____

3. During our teens, we would always watch *American Bandstand* after school. _____

4. When Louise and Kim were studying last night, Louise would crack her gum and drive Kim crazy. _____

5. Matthew would have finished college on time, but his mother contracted a serious illness, and his father needed him full-time in the family business for a year.

_____

Items 1, 2, and 5 are correct because each has a condition to be fulfilled. Items 3 and 4 are incorrect because neither one involves any notion of a condition to be fulfilled. Try to correct the problems in verb tense in 3 and 4.

EXERCISE 6.7

Underline all verbs and verb phrases. Then correct any examples of inconsistent or illogical verb tense.

1. Several years ago, experts in preventive medicine announced newly found reasons why fish is such an important element in a healthy diet.

2. It was common knowledge that fish was high in protein and low in fat, and for that reason, fish would always be a favorite with the diet-conscious.

3. But it turned out that fish has other benefits, too.

4. Perhaps surprisingly, the varieties of fish that could have been considered relatively high in calories when compared with other fish were the ones most enthusiastically recommended by nutritionists.

5. The so-called fatty fish varieties contained a very beneficial oil, which is made up of something called omega-3 fatty acids.

6. What can these fatty fish oils do for you? According to scientists, they had the power to lower your risk of heart disease, and they offered a certain amount of protection against the agonies of arthritis and asthma.

7. They would also quite possibly reduce the risk of breast cancer, but that is a benefit that scientists would need to research in more depth and over a longer period of time.

8. The fish that have enough oil to be recommended highly are tuna, herring, salmon, whitefish, and large bluefish.

9. Shad, mackerel, and pompano would also be included.

10. People who are concerned about calories should not avoid these varieties of fish; they are "fatty" only when compared with other types of fish.

11. A serving of Chinook salmon, for instance, at 180 calories per three-and-a-half-ounce portion, had more than twice the calories of a similar serving of sole, but it would have only half the calories that were in three-and-a-half ounces of beefsteak.

12. Fortunately, shrimp and lobster are also high in omega-3 fatty acids, and they are not nearly as high in cholesterol as nutrition experts previously had thought.

13. So fish might not be brain food, but it's a pretty smart thing to eat.

6.4 Apostrophes

Apostrophes (') are used in two ways: to show possession and to make contractions. We'll spend most of this unit working on possession.

Possession

An apostrophe is added to a noun to show that the noun owns something. For example, if a girl has her own room, you might refer to it as *the girl's room.* Notice that two nouns are involved: *girl* and *room.* The apostrophe is added to the noun that possesses (owns) the other.

In the phrase *the girl's room,* the letter *s* is also added to the word *girl.* But if we were referring to a room shared by *two* girls, the correct form would be *the girls' room.* The apostrophe would be placed *after* the *s.* In the latter example, the *s* is already part of the word because we're talking about two girls, not one girl. When a plural word already ends in *s* before it becomes possessive, you add only the apostrophe.

In other words, ask yourself, "Who owns the room?" If the answer is *the girl,* then you have a word that ends in the letter *l,* so you add an apostrophe plus -*s.* But if the answer to the question is *the two girls,* a word that already ends in -*s,* then you add only the apostrophe.

Make these into possessive phrases:

1. the voice of the singer = _____

2. the voices of the four singers = _____

3. the fleas belonging to one dog = _____

4. the fleas belonging to twelve dogs = _____

1. the singer's voice; 2. the four singers' voices; 3. one dog's fleas; 4. twelve dog's fleas.

Plural Words That Do Not End in -S

Sometimes the plural words that end in letters other than *s* give students trouble, but they really shouldn't. These words follow the same rule just described. In other words, whether something belongs to one *man* or to two *men,* you'll show possession in the same way—by adding -*'s.* Why? Because neither *man* nor *men* already ends in -*s* before you make it possessive. They both end in *n.* These are correct examples: *the man's*

Better Sentence-Writing

motive, the men's motive, the woman's car, the women's cars.
This rule holds true for all the plural nouns that end in *-men*
and for nouns such as *people, children, mice,* and *geese.*

Exercise 6.8

Write sentences in which you make possessive phrases from
the following. Add an apostrophe or an apostrophe plus *-s* as
needed. Use your own paper, please.

1. the duties of one librarian
   the duties of two librarians

2. the excitement of the child
   the excitement of the children

3. the shoes of the dancer
   the shoes of both dancers

4. the pet chameleon of one boy
   the pet chameleons of three boys

5. the history of the family
   the histories of the two families

6. the schedule of the woman
   the schedules of the women

7. the images of the poet
   the images of many poets

8. the carrots belonging to one rabbit
   the carrots belonging to all the rabbits

9. the performance of one drummer
   the performance of the drummers

10. the trips of the businessman
    the trips of the businessmen

Exercise 6.9

Change these phrases into ones that require an apostrophe or an apostrophe plus -*s*. For example:

The personality of my brother = my brother's personality

1. the priorities of the mayor = _____
2. the training of the pilots = _____
3. the comic talents of Jerry Seinfeld = _____
4. the game plan of the coaches = _____
5. the ice-cream sandwiches of the vendor =
   _____
6. the toys belonging to the babies = _____
7. the agreement of the friends = _____
8. the voice of Whitney Houston = _____
9. the role of Rob Morrow in *Northern Exposure* =
   _____
10. the role of the clowns in the circus = _____

Two Important Notes About the Exercises

Some sentences in the next two exercises may contain no words that call for an apostrophe; other sentences may have more than one.

Make sure that you correct each exercise and analyze any errors before you proceed to the next one.

Exercise 6.10

Add apostrophes where they are needed. (If you underline the words to which you add the apostrophes, they'll be easier to find and correct.)

151

Better Sentence-Writing

1. What do people like to order when they go out to eat? That was the National Restaurant Associations question, and it asked researchers from NPD Research Inc. to find the answer by surveying the members of 12,800 households.

2. The research organizations national survey reached all parts of the United States, and the poilsters discovered that Americans top five restaurant food choices are French fries, hamburgers, salads, breads, and pizza.

3. But all the various regions of the country have their own special favorites when it comes to ordering in the nations cafés and restaurants.

4. In New England, for instance, restaurant diners top menu choices include heroes and subs, doughnuts and sweet rolls, and sandwiches made of egg salad, tuna salad, and chicken salad.

5. A typical New Yorkers order is likely to include—in addition to heroes, subs, and salad-type sandwiches— frozen yogurt, sherbet, and types of pasta other than spaghetti.

6. In the mountain states of Arizona, Colorado, Idaho, Montana, Nevada, New Mexico, Utah, and Wyoming, peoples favorites range from tacos, burritos, and enchiladas to chicken nuggets and ham and cheese sandwiches.

7. It is anyones guess as to why, but North Dakotans restaurant preferences are mostly on the soft side; mashed potatoes, ice cream, doughnuts, sweet rolls, pancakes, and waffles rated the highest.

8. In Alaska, California, Hawaii, Oregon, and Washington, residents first loves are burritos, enchiladas, tacos, taco salads, and Oriental foods.

9. When food lovers in the South Atlantic states eat out, they are most likely to order the following items from a restaurants menu: breakfast sandwiches, shellfish, potato skins, and chicken.

10. In Illinois, Indiana, Michigan, Ohio, and Wisconsin, restaurant customers tastes are likely to run to chili, French toast, cheese, roast beef, and barbecued ribs.

Exercise 6.11

Add apostrophes where they are needed.

1. A parents greatest fear is that some harm will come to his or her child.

2. Grace Hechinger addresses this fear in a book called *How to Raise a Street-Smart Child.*

3. Hechinger, the mother of two boys, is a journalist and an educator who has written extensively on womens concerns and issues of family life. She has collaborated with her husband on a number of projects; the couples list of coauthored books includes *Teenage Tyranny, The New York Times Guide to New York City Private Schools,* and *Growing Up in America.*

4. Hechingers how-to book on keeping children from becoming victims makes some interesting observations and offers a few unusual bits of advice for parents.

5. One problem that concerns the author is that many childrens training at home puts them at risk when they are outside the home.

Better Sentence-Writing

A Final Note on Possession

What you've learned in this unit is the simplest system for showing possession. But there are variations to the rules. For example, you usually add an -s to a one-syllable name that already ends in -s, such as *James*. (In other words, you write about *James's future*.) By adding the extra -s, you are supplying a guide to pronunciation. Your teacher may discuss this variation or other ones, but the basic rules you've learned in this unit are sufficient to meet the standards of most college teachers.

Contractions

Using apostrophes to make possessives is challenging for some students, but using them for their other purpose—making contractions—is easy.

A *contraction* is a shortened form of two words, and contractions are usually acceptable in informal speech and writing. (We use them freely in this book.) The only thing you have to remember is that the apostrophe is placed at the spot where one or more letters have been omitted. For example, *I am* becomes *I'm*, and *you have* becomes *you've*.

Make contractions of the following pairs of words:

you are = _____   are not = _____

could have = _____   he is = _____

were not = _____   I am = _____

you had = _____   I would = _____

did not = _____   was not = _____

she will = _____   who is = _____

it is = _____   would not = _____

they have = _____   were not = _____

are not = _____   there is = _____

had not = _____   have not = _____

should not = _____   can not = _____

Correct your answers by consulting a dictionary.

●●

6.5 Pronoun Problems
●●

There are a number of problems that pronouns can present for writers, but two are especially common: *agreement* and *case.* We'll take agreement first.

Pronoun-Antecedent Agreement

You know that subjects have to agree with verbs. Well, pronouns have to agree, too. They have to agree with the nouns that they replace and to which they refer. Those nouns are called *antecedents;* they are the words that appear first and are then replaced by pronouns. For example, if you're talking about Patrick, and after a while you start referring to Patrick as *he,* then *Patrick* is the antecedent, and *he* is the pronoun that takes the place of it and refers to it. *Patrick* and *he* agree because they are both singular. You also have agreement when both the noun antecedent and the pronoun that replaces it are plural. You have disagreement only when one is plural and the other singular. Here are examples of the error of pronoun-antecedent disagreement. Correct 1 through 3 to make the antecedents and the pronouns agree in number:

1. The mailman came late, but *they* always do on Mondays.

2. A student is very fortunate if *they* have a job waiting for them after graduation.

3. All the vetoes were in, but *it* didn't add up to a clear picture.

It's really very simple. Singular pronouns agree with singular nouns. Plural pronouns agree with plural nouns.

Avoiding *His* or *Her* When Possible

Sometimes it's better to change a noun than a pronoun. This is especially true if not changing the noun antecedent forces you to overuse an expression such as *he or she* or *his or her*. Sometimes it's unavoidable, and you have to use he or she (unless you prefer *he* or *she* alone). But most of the time, this awkward option can be avoided by making the antecedent noun plural. For example, it's acceptable to write, "A *student* should think seriously about *his or her* real interests," but it's preferable to write, "*Students* should think seriously about *their* real interests."

Singular Collective Nouns

When you're working on pronoun-antecedent agreement, it's important to remember that words such as *group, family, team,* and *association* are normally considered singular. Each collective noun refers to one entity even though it may bring to mind a number of people. Therefore, a team, for example, is considered an *it,* not a *they.*

Prepositional Phrases

Here, as elsewhere, you have to be careful about prepositional phrases. Writers sometimes produce mistakes in pronoun-antecedent agreement by making a pronoun agree with a word inside a prepositional phrase when it really agrees with the noun before the prepositional phrase. Look at this correct example:

ante.

The *number* (of people) who are sick with the flu is almost incredible, and medical authorities tell us that it is still rising.

We say *it is still rising*, not *they are still rising*, because the antecedent is the singular word *number*. In other words, the people are not rising; the number is rising.

This does not mean that an antecedent never agrees with a noun inside a prepositional phrase. For example, what is the antecedent of *their* in this correct example?

The location of the boys was not released until their parents had been notified.

You simply have to use your powers of logic to make sure that your pronouns and antecedents agree.

Exercise 6.12

Fill in the blank with the correct pronoun. Also write *ante.* (for antecedent) over the noun or noun phrase that agrees with the pronoun you choose.

1. Everyone has heard of the Medal of Honor; _____ *(it was / they were)* first awarded during the Civil War.

2. Every man, woman, and child in America should say "Thanks!" to the Hurley Machine Company because in 1907 _____ *(it / they)* came out with the very first electric washing machine.

3. Nikon cameras are the cameras that news photographers use most often. _____ *(It was / They were)* also immortalized in Paul Simon's song "Kodachrome."

4. The Salvation Army is ever hopeful. _____ *(It has / They have)* as _____ *(its / their)* slogan, "A man may be down, but he's never out."

5. The Neanderthal man was discovered in 1856; _____ *(he was / they were)* found in Germany.

6. Apparently neither Gary Player nor his son had any major objection to entering into serious competition with a member of _____ (his/their) own family. The Players were the first father and son to compete in the same U.S. Open golf tournament.

7. Ostrich eggs are not known for _____ (its/their) daintiness; in fact, if you happened to have one, it would take you four hours just to hardboil _____ (it/them).

8. As the ill-fated *Andrea Doria* sank, the orchestra continued to perform; in fact, the last song _____ (it/they) played was "Arrivederci Roma."

9. Paper straws were invented in 1886 by Marvin Stone. He made _____ (it/them) by rolling paraffin-coated paper by hand.

10. (a) The McDonald's fast-food empire is constantly coming up with something new to promote business and keep customers happy, but one of the smartest things _____ (it/they) ever did was to build indoor and outdoor playgrounds at many of _____ (its/their) restaurants.
    (b) The people at McDonald's are constantly coming up with something new to promote business and keep customers happy, but one of the smartest things _____ (it/they) ever did was to build indoor and outdoor playgrounds at many of _____ (its/their) restaurants.

Exercise 6.13

Fill in the blank with the correct pronoun. Also write *ante.* over the noun or noun phrase that agrees with the pronoun you choose.

---

1. The Elvis Presley memorial stamp was issued in 1993; _____ *(it was / they were)* worth twenty-nine cents.

2. The rulers of Great Britain hold a lease on Hong Kong, but _____ *(it will / they will)* lose control there when _____ *(it expires / they expire)* in 1997.

3. Herschel Walker led the U.S. Football League in rushing yardage in 1983, which was _____ *(its / their)* first season.

4. The Fairy Investigation Society has _____ *(its / their)* headquarters in Dublin, Ireland.

5. If kept as pets, tarantulas are supposedly intelligent enough to recognize _____ *(its / their)* masters.

Pronoun Case

The words *I* and *me* are two different cases of the same pronoun—the first-person singular pronoun. *He* and *him* are two cases of the same pronoun, and so are *she* and *her*. When pronouns are used alone, native speakers of English rarely make mistakes with them, but when they are used in combination with a noun, mistakes are common. These are called mistakes in pronoun case. Here's an illustration:

(a) *She* is a frisky little child. (correct)

(b) Christopher and *her* are frisky little children. (incorrect)

In (a), the word *she* is obviously correct; *she* is the right pronoun to use in the subject position. But in (b), the word *her* is used as a subject, along with the word *Christopher*. No native speaker would write, "*Her* is a frisky little child," but many native speakers would make the error that is represented in sentence (b).

Better Sentence-Writing

It's the act of pairing a pronoun with a noun that seems to make writers occasionally lose their bearings. To avoid errors in pronoun case, all you have to do is watch for the pairings and mentally omit the noun. Then see what pronoun sounds right if used alone. That's the case of the pronoun that is also correct when used in combination with a noun.

Sometimes when you perform this test of omitting the noun, you also have to make a slight adjustment in subject-verb agreement or in the general phrasing of the sentence. For example, in (b) when you mentally omit the words *Christopher and*, you move from a plural subject to a singular subject, so you also have to change *are* to *is*. Then you ask yourself if it sounds right to say "Her is" or "She is."

Exercise 6.14

Fill in each blank with the correct case of the pronoun.

1. When did you last write a letter to _____ *(he / him)* and Annie?

2. Cody and _____ *(her / she)* are coming to Milwaukee for a visit in the spring.

3. Why don't you allow the Joneses and _____ *(them / they)* to go ahead and file the suit?

4. My children and _____ *(I / me)* really should write a book together.

5. The Blue Devils and _____ *(us / we)* battled throughout the entire tournament.

6. I'd like to take a trip to Argentina with Grandma Rosie and _____ *(her / she)*.

7. We can't wait until the Sethneys and _____ *(they / them)* finally get here.

8. Is the box that just arrived for Robin and _____ *(I / me)*?

9. Jackie and _____ *(he / him)* met about a year ago at the bank where she worked.

10. The man was rather rude to my brother and _____ *(I / me)*.

●●●

6.6 Easily Confused Words
●●●

This unit is a brief review of some of the common word pairs that often cause trouble for writers. You also might know of others that cause you uncertainty.

It would not be difficult for you to make up your own exercises on pairs that are not found here; if you do so, ask your teacher or a friend to check your work.

Below are the pairs that we'll consider in this unit. You can see that some are homonyms (words that sound alike but have different meanings), and some are not.

1. a/an	11. it's/its
2. accept/except	12. passed/past
3. affect/effect	13. principal/principle
4. amount/number	14. than/then
5. bare/bear	15. their/there/they're
6. coarse/course	16. threw/through
7. conscience/conscious	17. to/too/two
8. finally/finely	18. weather/whether
9. have/of	19. who's/whose
10. hear/here	20. you're/your

___
161

Troublesome Pairs

1. A/An

A and *An* are both noun markers. *A* is used before words that begin with consonant sounds, and *an* is used before words that begin with vowel sounds. You probably remember that the vowels are *a, e, i, o,* and *u.* There are two more things you should know. One is that the letter *h* is sometimes silent, and when it is, you use *an.* For example, you write, "It is *an* honor to speak before the assembly." On the other hand, when *h* is sounded, you use a. For example, you might say, "I wonder if there is *a* heaven."

The other special concern is the letter *u.* Words that begin with a long *u* are preceded by *a;* words that begin with a short *u* are preceded by *an.* Study these correct examples: *a* united student body; *an* unsung hero.

2. Accept/Except

Accept is the verb form of the noun *acceptance,* and it means to receive something, not to reject it. The word *except* is a preposition that is related to the noun *exception.* Examples: You *accept* praise from your teacher. You might enjoy all dances *except* the polka.

3. Affect/Effect

If you look in a good dictionary, you'll find a complete explanation of the difference between these two words. For our purposes, it's enough to say that *affect* is a verb, and *effect* is usually a noun. Examples: Your moods *affect* your performance. The *effect* of too little sleep is obvious.

4. Amount/Number

Use the word *number* when you're writing about something that can be counted; use *amount* when you're writing about something that can't be counted. Examples: *an amount of peanut butter, a number of peanuts.* Use *number* if something is "countable," even if you don't know the exact count.

Most people don't make errors with *number;* they make errors by overusing *amount.* Here's a typical mistake: "I had a large *amount* of friends when I lived in Houston." Friends can be counted, even if you don't actually recall how many you had; therefore, it should be "I had a large *number* of friends."

The words *fewer* and *less* operate in the same way. *Fewer* is used as *number* is—with things that can be counted. *Less* is used as *amount* is—with things that can't be counted. Is the TV commercial that tells us one type of beer has "less calories" than another type grammatically correct? The answer is no.

The words *many* and *much* also operate similarly. *Many* is used with things that can be counted; *much* modifies things that can't be counted. Study these correct examples:

Can Be Counted	Cannot Be Counted
the number of jokes	the amount of humor
fewer jokes	less humor
many jokes	much humor

5. Bare/Bear

The word *bare* is an adjective that means naked, plain, unadorned. It is also a verb that means to reveal. *Bear* has two basic meanings: It's a noun that refers to a certain animal; it's also a verb that means to carry a burden or to tolerate something. Examples: The room is too *bare;* it needs a few warm touches. He wants to *bare* his soul to you. You may encounter a grizzly *bear* in Glacier National Park. I can't *bear* to think about final exam week.

6. Coarse/Course

The word *course* means an academic subject, such as a mathematics course. It also means a path or route, such as the course of a river or a golf course. *Course* means a duration, as in the expression "throughout the course of history." Its most frequent use is probably in the phrase *of course.*

163

Coarse, on the other hand, is an adjective that means rough; it can describe such things as the texture of fabric or the sound of language.

7. Conscience/Conscious

Conscience is a noun; it's what is supposed to bother you when you do something wrong; we could say it's your sense of right and wrong. The word *conscious* is an adjective that means aware. It's related to the noun *consciousness.* Examples: He had a guilty *conscience* after betraying his friend's trust. She was *conscious* of someone watching her.

8. Finally/Finely

Finally means at last or eventually. *Finely* means delicately or in small pieces.

9. Have/Of

This problem is a little different. Sometimes writers use the preposition *of* when they really mean the verb *have.* The only time this mistake occurs is after helping verbs such as *should, could, will, would, may, might,* and *must.* In the middle of a verb phrase, you don't want a preposition. Here's a typical error: "I should *of* known better." Here's the correction: "I should *have* known better."

10. Hear/Here

Hear is the verb that means listen. *Here* is an adverb that designates a place.

11. It's/Its

It's is the contraction of *it is.* The word *its* is a possessive pronoun. Examples: *It's* a new day. The snake shed *its* skin.

12. Passed/Past

Passed is a form of the verb *pass. Past* can be a noun or an adjective. Examples: They all *passed* the exam. You *passed* me on the street without saying a word. Who ever really forgets the *past?* (noun) Your *past* mistakes are forgiven. (adjective)

13. Principal/Principle

We all remember that the *principal* is our pal. The noun also refers to a sum of money on which we can earn interest. But the problem most students have is that they don't realize the word *principal* is also an adjective that means main, central, most important. The word *principle* is a noun that means a basic truth, a law, a rule, a belief, a standard, or an ideal. Examples: Solving world hunger is the *principal* goal of the organization. Ozzie's *principal* problem is lack of confidence. This experiment demonstrates the *principle* of supply and demand. Charlie has no *principles;* he'll do anything for a price.

14. Than/Then

Than is used to make comparisons. For example, a person can be stronger *than* someone else, and one climate can be warmer *than* another. *Then* is an adverb of time; it describes when an action occurred. For example, we say, "*Then* I woke up" and "If you decide you want to talk it over, *then* call me."

15. Their/There/They're

Their is a possessive pronoun. It modifies a noun by showing that the noun belongs to someone. We speak of *their pencils, their cars, their future.* *There* is an indicator of location, as in "Let's go *there* now." It is also a sort of meaningless sentence starter, as in "*There* are a few problems we need to discuss." *They're* is the contraction of *they are*, as in "*They're* going to be here for an hour."

16. Threw/Through

Threw is the past tense of the verb *throw*. *Through* is a preposition.

Better Sentence-Writing

17. To/Too/Two

To can be part of an infinitive verb phrase, as in "She wants *to* ride." *To* is also a preposition, as in "The poem *to* his daughter was never completed." *Two,* of course, is the number between one and three. It's *too* that gives writers the most trouble. *Too* is an "intensifier"; it makes the adjective that follows it more intense. Roughly, it means "excessively." For example, you can say, "You are *too* impatient," which means you are excessively impatient. *Too* has another meaning, which is "also." For example, you can write, "Please clean up this mess, and do the dishes, *too.*"

18. Weather/Whether

Weather, of course, refers to the climate. *Whether* is a conjunction used in sentences such as "I don't know *whether* I should sign up now or wait until tomorrow."

19. Who's/Whose

Who's is the contraction of *who is. Whose* is a possessive pronoun, and you've worked with it as an embedding word.

20. You're/Your

You're is the contraction of *you are. Your* is a possessive pronoun.

Exercise 6.15

Fill in the blanks with the correct choices.

1. Reindeer's milk has three times more protein _____ *(than/then)* cow's milk, and some people prefer the taste, _____ *(to/too/two).*

2. The _____ *(principal/principle)* center of diamond trading in the United States is New York City's 47th Street; in fact, more _____ *(than/then)* 75 percent of the action in the American diamond trade goes on _____ *(their/there/they're).*

3. Richard Nixon was the first person _____
   (to/too/two) put a telephone call _____
   (threw/through) to the moon.

4. The _____ *(principal/principle)* of self-service,
   which of _____ *(coarse/course)* had a negative
   _____ *(affect/effect)* on the employment of a
   great _____ *(amount/number)* of waiters
   and waitresses, goes all the way back _____
   (to/too/two) 1885 when the first self-service restaurant, the Exchange Buffet, opened _____
   (it's/its) doors near the New York Stock Exchange.

5. Joe Louis, _____ *(who's/whose)* considered
   by many to be the greatest fighter who ever lived,
   held the heavyweight title longer _____
   (than/then) anyone else; if _____
   (you're/your) up on _____ *(you're/your)*
   boxing trivia, you know that he was the champion
   from 1937 _____ *(to/too/two)* 1949.

6. Each of the precisely etched, _____ *(finally/
   finely)* carved faces of the presidents at Mt.
   Rushmore is _____ *(to/too/two)* times higher
   _____ *(than/then)* the Great Sphinx of Egypt.

7. The Eighteenth Amendment, which prohibited the
   sale of liquor in the United States, was the only one
   ever to be repealed. The American people
   _____ *(finally/finely)* _____
   (threw/through) the amendment out on December 5,
   1933, after almost 14 "dry years" had _____
   (passed/past). Apparently, they came to the conclusion
   that, for adults, drinking alcohol should be considered less a matter of legislation _____
   (than/then) a matter of individual _____
   (conscience/conscious).

8. The first American husband and wife team to
   _____ *(accept/except)* the Nobel Prize was

Better Sentence-Writing

Dr. Carl F. Cori and Dr. Gerty T. Cori. _____
(Their / There / They're) work in medicine won them a
joint prize in 1947.

9. The United States publishes a greater _____
   (amount / number) of newspapers _____
   (than / then) any other country.

10. _____ *(It's / Its)* a fact that _____
    (their / there / they're) are exactly twenty possible first
    moves in chess.

11. If _____ *(you're / your)* ever watching a tele-
    vision sitcom and the laughter seems just a bit
    _____ *(to / too / two)* mechanical, it might
    _____ *(have / of)* been produced by a
    machine called a "Mackenzie." _____
    (It's / Its) job is to cough up canned laughter for a con-
    siderable _____ *(amount / number)* of televi-
    sion shows.

12. Throughout the entire _____ *(coarse / course)*
    of American history, _____ *(their / there / they're)*
    was probably only one president who didn't let his
    spouse's views _____ *(affect / effect)* his politi-
    cal decisions in even the slightest way. That was
    James Buchanan, who served from 1857 to 1861 and
    who was the only American president never
    _____ *(to / too / two)* marry.

13. By the standards of centuries ago, it didn't really take
    _____ *(to / too / two)* long for the Mayflower
    to cross the Atlantic; in fact, the ship left Europe and
    arrived _____ *(hear / here)* in only _____
    (to / too / two) months.

14. The presidential candidate who received the greatest
    _____ *(amount / number)* of votes in one
    election in American history was Richard M. Nixon.
    But he must _____ *(bare / bear)* the stigma

of being the only president to resign, _____
(to / too / two).

15. During the time of the Civil War, _____
(their / there / they're) was no doubt that money could
_____ *(affect / effect)* a young man's chances
of serving in the military; to put it plainly, _____
(a / an) inductee could pay someone else _____
(to / too / two) take his place if, of _____
(coarse / course), he could do so without disturbing his
own _____ *(conscience / conscious)* _____
(to / too / two) much.

••

6.7 Capitalization
••

There are many fine points of capitalization, but these basic
guidelines will meet most of the needs of college writers. The
following categories of words are capitalized:

1. **Titles of poems, short stories, plays, books,
   newspapers, magazines, television shows, radio
   programs, and movies.** Capitalize the first and last
   word and every other word with the exception of coordinating conjunctions, prepositions, articles (*a, an,*
   and *the*) and the word *to* in infinitive verb phrases.
   (Titles of poems, short stories, and individual television and radio programs are also enclosed within double quotation marks; titles of books, newspapers,
   magazines, films, and television and radio series are
   normally italicized.)

   Correct examples: "The Love Song of J. Alfred
   Prufrock," "Air and Angels," "Delight in Disorder,"
   "On the Death of Dr. Robert Levet," *Murphy Brown,
   Sesame Street, The Valley of Horses, The Milwaukee
   Journal, Pro Football Digest, One Flew Over the*

169

Cuckoo's Nest, Butch Cassidy and the Sundance Kid, On the Waterfront.

2. **Brand names.** Brand names are always capitalized.

Correct examples: Bisquick buttermilk baking mix, Nike running shoes, Clinique cosmetics, Arrow shirts, Sylvania light bulbs, Head & Shoulders shampoo.

3. **Breeds of animals.** Capitalize the name of a breed of animal if it is derived from another proper (capitalized) noun. The names that are capitalized below are derived from the names of nationalities, which are always capitalized. Use your dictionary if you are in doubt.

Correct examples: alley cat, Persian cat, Old English sheepdog, beagle, French poodle, quarter horse, Arabian horse.

4. **Buildings and institutions.** The names of buildings and institutions are always capitalized.

Correct examples: the White House, the Taj Mahal, the Superdome, St. Joseph's Hospital, the University of Iowa, the Berkeley Psychic Institute.

5. **Companies and corporations.** The names of companies and corporations are always capitalized.

Correct examples: Colgate-Palmolive Company, Mobil Oil Corporation, Lockheed Aircraft Corporation.

6. **Days of the week.** The days of the week are always capitalized.

Correct examples: Monday, Tuesday.

7. **Directions.** The names of directions are normally *not* capitalized. Capitalize them only when they name or modify an entire region—a whole section of a country or a continent.

Correct examples: I live four miles west of the lake. Her study covered the era when the South was at war with the North.

8. **Geographical locations and words derived from them.** All of these are capitalized: the names of cities, counties, states, nations, lakes, rivers, oceans, mountain ranges, parks, continents, and planets.

   Correct examples: Seattle, Washington, Blue Lake, the Atlantic Ocean, the Allegheny Mountains, France, Jupiter, Mars.

   Two special notes: Most words that are derived from these location words are capitalized; for example, *Switzerland* is capitalized, and so is *Swiss* cheese. The word *Mexico* is capitalized, and so is *Mexican* art.

   Normally, the word *earth* is not capitalized, but when it refers to the entire planet, it is. *These are correct examples:* The earth in some parts of the country has a reddish color. The Earth is not the largest planet that revolves around the sun.

9. **Historical periods.** Names of historical periods are usually capitalized. If you are in doubt, consult your dictionary.

   Correct examples: the Renaissance, the Pleistocene Age, the Middle Ages.

10. **Holidays.** The names of holidays and holy days are always capitalized.

    Correct examples: Christmas, Yom Kippur, Thanksgiving.

11. The word *I* is always capitalized.

12. **Months of the year.** The months of the year are always capitalized.

    Correct examples: January, February, March.

171

A special note: Although the months are capitalized, the seasons are usually not. Capitalize the name of a season only if it is part of the formal name of something else, such as a dance or a celebration of some sort. *These are correct examples:* I won't see you again until next winter. Our school's famous Fall Festival was only a modest financial success this year, but the Spring Fling will probably be a bigger money-maker.

13. **Mother and father.** Mistakes are often made in capitalizing or not capitalizing person nouns such as *mother, father, mom,* and *dad.* But the rule is really very simple: Do not capitalize these words when they are preceded by a possessive noun or pronoun. *Study these correct examples:*

   (a) I have always considered *Dad* a perfectionist.
   I have always considered *my dad* a perfectionist.

   (b) I met *Father* at the restaurant.
   I met *my neighbor's father* at the restaurant.

14. **Names of people and pets.** Names of people and pets are always capitalized.

   Correct examples: Maya Angelou, Sarah Zeilman, John Brown, Snoopy, Fluffy, Killer.

15. **One-of-a-kind events.** Large one-of-a-kind or once-a-year events are normally capitalized.

   Correct examples: the Orange Bowl, the World Series, the War of 1812.

16. **Organizations and associations.** The names of organizations and associations are capitalized. Once again, articles, coordinating conjunctions, and prepositions are not capitalized.

Correct examples: American Civil Liberties Union, Children's Literature Association, National Aeronautics and Space Administration, National Council of Teachers of English.

17. **Political parties.** The names of political parties and words derived from them are capitalized. (Note, however, that the word party is not.)

Correct examples: the Republican party, the Democratic candidate, the Socialist platform, the Communists.

18. **Religions.** The names of religions and words derived from them are capitalized.

Correct examples: the Jewish people, the Protestants' representative, the Mormons, the Baptist minister.

19. **The first word in a sentence.** The first word of a new sentence is capitalized, and this is also true of quoted sentences that are a part of larger sentences.

Correct examples: The note said, "Your books have been overdue for a month. Please return them and pay your fine."

20. **Personal titles.** Personal titles are capitalized only when they directly precede a person's name or when they are used as a form of direct address. This is true for words such as president, general, mayor, doctor, king, queen, professor, dean, and pope.

Correct examples: Do you realize that President Clinton's press conference is on television right now? Do you realize that the president's press conference is on television right now? The reporter asked, "When did you first know of this situation, Mr. President?"

Better Sentence-Writing

Correct the following sentences, applying what you've learned about capitalization.

1. Experts at the new york museum of modern art, after studying french artist henri matisse's le bateau for more than six weeks, discovered that the painting had been hung upside down.

2. Geoffrey chaucer once wrote, "love is blind," and william shakespeare used that line, too.

3. The lincoln memorial in washington, d.c., has 36 columns.

4. Ernest hemingway, the great american novelist who gave us *the sun also rises, a farewell to arms, for whom the bell tolls, the old man and the sea,* and other important works, was supposedly very reluctant to travel on fridays.

5. It was in a movie called *sudden impact* that clint eastwood first said, "make my day."

6. The best selling car in history was the volkswagen beetle.

7. Three of every four russian doctors are women.

8. It was once suggested by president jimmy carter that each president be elected for a single six-year term of office.

9. In the frontier days of the west, cheyenne, wyoming, was nicknamed "hell on wheels."

10. John lindsay, a former mayor of new york city, made his acting debut in the movie *rosebud* in 1975.

Answer Key

Chapter 1 Answer Key

If some of your answers for the exercises in this unit vary a bit from those shown, your answers are not necessarily wrong. When marking clauses, you may have included slightly more or less than is shown here; such differences are inconsequential and to be expected.

Exercise 1.1

1. *s* = motive; *v* = was; *sub com* = mysterious
2. *s* = I; *v* = bought; *do* = suit
3. *s* = woman; *v* = coughed
4. *s* = Caroline; *v* = gave; *io* = Steven; *do* = choice
5. *s* = nectarines; *v* = feel; *sub com* = ripe

Exercise 1.2

1. *s* = fans; *v* = consider; *do* = Nolan Ryan; *ob com* = pitcher
2. *s* = pitcher; *v* = shows; *io* = hitters; *do* = best stuff
3. *s* = season; *v* = was; *sub com* = twenty-fourth
4. *s* = fastballs; *v* = reached; *do* = speeds
5. *s* = fastball; *v* = made; *do* = curveball; *ob com* = more effective

Exercise 1.3

1. beginning
2. prediction
3. organization
4. liar
5. gentleness
6. decision

Better Sentence-Writing

7. allowance
8. reliability
9. collection
10. defiance

Exercise 1.4

1. *s* = To work hard today
2. *s* = What the world needs now
3. *s* = Tracking students into so-called ability groups
4. *s* = Outside that crazy office
5. *s* = What a racist or sexist joke reveals about its teller

Exercise 1.5

1. *s* = deprivation; *v* = can prevent; *do* = retention
2. *s* = tongue; *v* = has given; *io* = doctors; *do* = mirror
3. *s* = Malcolm X; *v* = had made; do trips; *v* = had altered; *do* = position
4. *s* = *Nintendo Power* magazine; *v* = is published
5. *s* = Vincent van Gogh; *v* = painted; *do* = suns; *ob com* = yellow
6. *s* = Competition; *v* = has been defined
7. *s* = Chester F. Carlson; *v* = should have named; *do* = intervention; *ob com* = after himself
8. *s* = mannequins; *v* = wear; *do* = size 40 regular

9. *s* = size; *v* = has been decreasing
10. *s* = people; *v* = should blame; *do* = diet

Exercise 1.6

1. polished, oak
2. biggest, small
3. negative, best
4. deep, raspy
5. persistent, drastic
6. supporting, historical
7. crystal, big
8. tallest, old-fashioned, blackberry
9. final, difficult, challenging
10. dramatic, sunburnt, pale, white

Exercise 1.7

In each answer for this exercise, the words between the commas form the appositive, and the labeled parts of the clause form the kernel.

1. George Washington, the first president of the United States, loved peanut soup.
   s = George Washington; *v* = loved; *do* = peanut soup
2. John Quincy Adams, the sixth president, liked swimming nude in the Potomac River every morning at five o'clock.
   s = John Quincy Adams; *v* = liked; *do* = swimming

176

3. Zachary Taylor, a career officer in the army for most of his life, voted for the first time at the age of 62.
   s = Zachary Taylor; *v* = voted

4. James Buchanan, president from 1857 to 1861, was a bachelor throughout his entire life.
   s = James Buchanan; *v* = was; *sub com* = bachelor

5. Abraham Lincoln, an extremely persistent individual, won the presidency in 1860 after eight election losses in a row.
   s = Abraham Lincoln; *v* = won; *do* = presidency

Exercise 1.8

After you have crossed out the prepositional phrases and other modifiers, the remaining components that form the kernels are these:

1. *s* = Robin Burns; *v* = is; *sub com* = officer; *App.:* the highest paid woman in the United States
2. *s* = Babe Ruth; *v* = pitched
3. *s* = number; *v* = exceeded; *do* = number
4. *s* = color; *v* = has been; *sub com* = blue
5. *s* = Treasury Department; *v* = dry-cleaned; *do* = money
6. *s* = female tree frog; *v* = recognizes; *do* = connection

7. *s* = headquarters; *v* = has; *do* = waterbed
8. *s* = matter; *v* = is; *sub com* = duff
9. *s* = size; *v* = was; *sub com* = 5 feet and 7 inches and 135 pounds
10. *s* = record; *v* = was; *sub com* = I'll Never Get Out of this World Alive"

Chapter 2 Answer Key

Exercise 2.1

1. *s* = Mexican-Americans; *v* = have; *do* = families *s* = they; *v* = can claim; *do* = rate United States, and they
2. *s* = gardeners; *v* = wanted; *do* = melons *s* = they; *v* = watered; *do* = them melons, so they
3. *s* = tissues; *v* = are; *sub com* = great; *s* = sheets; *v* = were invented sufferers, but those
4. *s* = Wilson and Smith; *v* = had; *do* = problem; *s* = they; *v* = joined; *do* = forces; *v* = started; *do* = Alcoholics Anonymous problem, so they
5. *s* = people; *v* = keep; *do* = resolutions; *s* = they; *v* = don't make; *do* = them weeks, or they

Better Sentence-Writing

Exercise 2.2

1. *s* = you; *v* = lick; *do* = stamp
   s = you; *v* = consume; *do* = one-tenth
   Conj. = When
   stamp, you

2. *s* = birth; *v* = created; *do* = sensation
   s = set; *v* = had survived
   Conj. = because
   no punctuation added

3. *s* = Pretty Boy Floyd; *v* = was known
   Conj. = Although
   robberies, he

4. *s* = people; *v* = must live *s* = government; *v* calls; *do* = it;
   ob com = city
   Conj. = before
   no punctuation added

5. *s* = Fitzgerald; *v* = had completed; *do* = *The Last Tycoon*
   s = it; *v* = might have been;
   sub com = novel
   Conj. = If
   44, it

Exercise 2.3

1. Thomas Jefferson, who was certainly one of America's most brilliant presidents, was broke when he died.

2. Monrovia, which is the capital of the West African nation of Liberia, was founded in 1822 and named after President James Monroe.

3. Herbert Hoover, who once gave an order that no White House staffers were to pet his dog, was supposedly worried that King Tut was becoming too attached to other people.

4. James Buchanan, whose 23-year-old fiancé broke off their engagement and died mysteriously a short time later, was the only president to remain a bachelor.

5. Grover Cleveland's duties as a sheriff in New York State, which included serving as one county's official hangman, resulted in his participation in the execution of two convicted murderers.

Exercise 2.4

1. *Reduced:* A quetzal, unable to take off into the air like other birds, has to jump off a tree branch backward to avoid snagging its 24-inch tail.

   Moved: Unable to take off into the air like other birds, a quetzal has to jump off a tree branch backward to avoid snagging its 24-inch tail.

2. *Reduced:* Male narwhals, nicknamed "unicorns of the sea," sport a single nine-foot-long tusk.

   Moved: Nicknamed "unicorns of the sea," male narwhals sport a single nine-foot-long tusk.

178

3. *Reduced:* Some biologists, puzzled by the hump on the back of the thorny devil, speculate that the lizard can push the hump up to create the illusion of a second head when it wants to confuse its enemies.

Moved: Puzzled by the hump on the back of the thorny devil, some biologists speculate that the lizard can push the hump up to create the illusion of a second head when it wants to confuse its enemies.

4. *Reduced:* A sloth, blessed with three very efficient curved claws on each foot, normally hangs from a tree for its daily 18-hour snooze.

Moved: Blessed with three very efficient curved claws on each foot, a sloth normally hangs from a tree for its daily 18-hour snooze.

5. *Reduced:* One scientist, curious about the basic color of the zebra, conducted a study and concluded that zebras are actually black with white stripes, not white with black stripes.

Moved: Curious about the basic color of the zebra, one scientist conducted a study and concluded that zebras are actually black with white stripes, not white with black stripes.

Exercise 2.5

Possible revisions for the run-on sentences are offered here. You may have come up with different revisions.

1. RO; them/this
   For over 2,700 years, diamonds have had a certain mystique.

2. CS; India,/they
   The first diamonds were discovered along riverbeds in south central India in about 800 B.C.

3. CS; years,/then;
   source,/later South central India was the primary source of diamonds for about two thousand years. Then, South America became the major source; later, South Africa was the major source.

4. OK

5. CS; mines,/most
   There are 19 diamond mines in the United States, most of which are around the border between Colorado and Wyoming.

Exercise 2.6

1. OK

2. CS; three C's,/the
   Diamonds are judged on the basis of the three C's: carats, cut, and clarity.

3. RO; "carob seed"/carob
   The word carat comes from

179

Better Sentence-Writing

the Greek word keration,
which means "carob seed."
Carob seeds were used to
measure the weight of
diamonds long ago in India.

4. RO; measure/it
In the modern world of
diamond dealing, a carat,
which represents ¹/₁₄₂ of an
ounce, is a more standard
measure.

5. CS; carats,/that
The largest diamond ever
found was 3,106 carats,
which equals about 1.3
pounds.

Exercise 2.7

1. F
The Statistical Abstract,
which is produced annually
by the U.S. Commerce
Department, fills almost
1,000 pages.

2. OK

3. F
Massachusetts, for example,
is the state with the highest
number of doctors per
100,000 people.

4. F
New York has more lawyers
per person than any other
state.

5. OK

Exercise 2.8

1. F
Cross Your Fingers, Spit in
Your Hat is a book about
superstitions and folklore.

2. F
The most interesting
superstitions are the ones
about love and marriage.

3. OK

4. OK

5. F
The object of your desire will
also love you if you give him
or her a bowl of soup that is
flavored with three drops of
your blood.

Chapter 3 Answer Key

Exercise 3.1

1. Complex
Conj. = When
1919, Handley Page
Transport; s = it; v =
introduced; do = box lunches
s = Handley Page Transport;
v = became; sub com = airline

2. Complex
Conj. = when
no punctuation added; s = no
one; v = was; sub com =
surprised; s = Wilma P.
Mankiller; v = became; sub
com = chief

3. Compound
Conj. = but
cans, but; s = drinkers;

v = buy; *do* = beer; s = beer; v = outsold; *do* = beer

4. Complex
Conj. = after
no punctuation added; s = Queen Victoria; v = wore; *do* = in black; s = she; v = lost; *do* = husband or Albert or husband Albert

5. Complex
Conj. = since
48, the royalties; s = Gibran; v = died; s = royalties; v = have helped; *do* = people

Exercise 3.2

1. s = St. Nicholas
St. Nicholas, **who was a fourth-century bishop in Asia Minor,** is the patron saint of children and sailors.

2. s = The dog who guarded the gates of Hades
no punctuation should be added

3. s = Janet Reno
Janet Reno, **who became U.S. Attorney General shortly before the cult-related tragedy in Texas,** was praised ... decisions.

4. s = The person who wrote the Oz books
no punctuation should be added

5. s = The average child who is between two and three years of age

no punctuation should be added

Exercise 3.3

1. s = A person
no punctuation should be added

2. s = The person
no punctuation should be added

3. s = The U.S. Senate
The U.S. Senate, **which has been called "the most exclusive club in the world,"** is never open to more than 100 members.

4. s = The grape
no punctuation should be added

5. s = The abbreviation *lb.*
The abbreviation *lb.*, **which means pound,** comes from the Latin word *libra,* meaning "scales."

Exercise 3.4

1. Chubby Checker, whose real name was Ernest Evans, worked as a chicken plucker in a poultry shop before he became famous for doing "The Twist."

2. Neil Sedaka, who had enjoyed a great deal of success as a songwriter and singer in the 1950s, made a comeback in the 1970s with the help of Elton John.

3. Critic Jon Landau, who wrote a rave review after seeing "the Boss" in concert in 1974, is responsible for the line "I saw rock 'n' roll's future, and its name is Bruce Springsteen."

4. Annie Mae Bullock, who married Ike Turner in 1958, changed her name to Tina Turner.

5. The heart attack that left Jackie Wilson in a coma for the rest of his life occurred while the famous soul singer was performing on stage in Cherry Hill, New Jersey, on September 25, 1975.

Exercise 3.5

1. racetrack, a maiden
2. American Revolution, the Purple Heart
3. years, having
4. 1918, followed
5. *khaki,* meaning

Exercise 3.6

1. ducks, swans, geese, eagles, foxes, wolves, and
2. *Fly patterns, flares, bombs, safety blitzes,* and
3. 164 feet high, 148 feet wide, and
4. wisdom, wealth, power, and
5. Ariel, Miranda, Oberon, Titania, and

Exercise 3.7

1. (a) quick little smile
   (b) generous, good-hearted smile
2. (a) serious military affair
   (b) ridiculous, tragic affair
3. (a) perfect tea roses
   (b) delicate, delightful roses
4. (a) creamy, buttery soup
   (b) delicious bean soup
5. (a) skillful, thoughtful sculptor
   (b) thoughtful Italian sculptor

Exercise 3.8

1. Timbuktu, you'll
   Timbuktu, which ... gold, was settled
2. sundae, now ... treat, was ... parlor, and
3. October 25, 1940, Col. B.O. Davis
4. 1886, John Styth Pemberton, an Atlanta pharmacist, will
5. light up, they experts, male
6. France, who ... old, is credited
7. fused, eroded
   Desert roses, which ... elements, are
8. Cicero, not George Washington
9. bread, a sweetbread
10. longest, heaviest ... python, a typical

Exercise 3.9

1. track; she
2. structure; it
3. bone; they
4. full-time job; high school girls
5. riflemen; oarsmen

Exercise 3.10

1. Caspian Sea; however, the
2. East; the less
3. *The Gambler*;—in fact, the
4. three inches; consequently, the
5. injury; for example, if
6. copyrighted work; in fact, it
7. hair; the wife
8. *Casablanca;* however, few people
9. bad luck; a talisman
10. amulets; a four-leaf clover

Exercise 3.11

1. (a) no punctuation should be added
   (b) His idea, however, was
   (c) great idea; however, it
2. (a) Ben's; in fact, she
   (b) no punctuation should be added
   (c) She was, in fact, his
3. (a) no punctuation should be added
   (b) is, therefore, going
   (c) engineering; therefore, he

4. (a) no punctuation should be added
   (b) children; for example, some
   (c) youngsters, for example, speak
5. (a) no punctuation should be added
   (b) choice; on the other hand, John is afraid
   (c) John, on the other hand, thinks

Exercise 3.12

Only the parts of each item requiring additional punctuation appear here.

1. Those periods are the following: between three and ten months, between two and four years, between six and eight years, between 10 and 12 years, and between 14 and 16 years. *sub com* = the following
2. Santa's eight tiny reindeer are Dasher, Dancer, Prancer, Vixen, Comet, Cupid, Donner, and Blitzen.
3. These are the seven wonders of the ancient world: the Great Pyramid of Cheops, the Hanging Gardens of Babylon, the Tomb of King Mausolus at Halicarnassus, the Temple of Artemis, the Colossus of Rhodes, the Statue of Zeus at Olympia, and the lighthouse

on the Isle of Pharos.
sub com = wonders

4. But those who want to be more precise might use one of these terms: a bevy of quail, a muster of peacocks, a charm of finches, or an exaltation of larks.
do = one (or one of these terms)

5. Charles Biondin, the French acrobat and tightrope walker, crossed Niagara Falls in 1855, 1859, and 1860.

Exercise 3.13

1. *Sea of Slaughter,* which ... Press, was
2. Mowat, who is a Canadian, is
3. seaboard, Mowat
4. area, his conclusions
5. author, human beings ... mammals, birds, and fish of North America; in fact, Mowat
6. reasons: economic, recreational, and scientific
7. meat, hides, and fur
8. survived, but ... difficulty; for example, the wolf, the Plains buffalo, and
9. animals, such as the passenger pigeon, the sea mink, and the Eastern buffalo, are gone forever, driven into
10. harsh, tragic realities, and ... history; animals ... for sport,

for fashion, for food, and for experimentation

Exercise 3.14

1. *Sea of Slaughter, a* ... 400 pages, points out
2. people, for example, believe
3. bird, which ... hour, did exist
4. 100 million, its natural
5. That enemy, of course, was deadly; it was man.
6. whale, once ... life forms, is
7. odds: the coyote
8. no additional punctuation necessary
9. predator, Mowat ... future, but ... individuals, not
10. rare, they ... sensitive, aware publication, it

Chapter 4 Answer Key

Exercise 4.1

The sample rewrites given here are not the only possibilities. You may have come up with other good revisions.

1. OK; *s* = beer
2. OK; *s* = hard candies and caramels
3. DM; *s* = U.S. Army
According to the U.S. Army, an M-1 rifle that is cared for properly should last 10,000 rounds.

4. DM; *s* = scientists
   Scientists believe that the sun, which is four to five billion years old, has a life span of 10 billion years.

5. DM; *s* = plastic surgeons
   Plastic surgeons estimate that a successful face lift performed upon average skin should last from six to 10 years.

Exercise 4.2

The following sample rewrites are not the only possibilities. You may have come up with other good revisions.

1. DM; *s* = Southeast Asia
   Southeast Asia is the home of the world's largest bat, which can weigh up to 32 ounces and which has a wingspan that's been measured at five feet, seven inches.

2. OK; *s* = basenji dog

3. DM; *s* = it
   Swans, which are extremely long-lived, can survive up to one hundred years.

4. OK; *s* = goliath beetle

5. DM; *s* = zoos
   Some zoos have black and white Bengal tigers that lack the tiger's usual reddish orange coloring. The Bengais are all descendants of a single white male tiger named Bohan, who was found in a jungle in India around the middle of this century.

Exercise 4.3

These sample rewrites are not the only possible corrections. You may have come up with other strong revisions.

1. (a) In addition, if the teachers of the future are to come from the best class of students, they will need higher salaries, greater professional status, and more opportunities for advancement.

   (b) In addition, if the teachers of the future are to come from among the best students, educators will need to earn more money, enjoy greater professional status, and have more opportunities for advancement.

2. (a) Seasoned travelers suggest that you take a daytime flight, eat as little as possible on the plane, and nap as much as you can while in the air.

   (b) The suggestions of seasoned travelers include taking a daytime flight, eating as little airline food as possible, and napping as much as you can while you're in the air.

3. (a) The child who is ready for kindergarten should be able

to name at least three or four colors, draw or copy a square, repeat a series of four numbers without practice, tell the right hand from the left, and identify what things such as cars, chairs, and shoes are made of.

(b) If children can name three or four colors, draw or copy a square, repeat four numbers in a row without practice, tell their right hand from their left, and identify what such items as cars, chairs, and shoes are made of, then they are probably ready to start kindergarten.

Exercise 4.4

Here are possible rewrites; yours may differ.

1. The baby calf of a blue whale gains approximately 200 pounds per day.
2. Goldfish in captivity have reached the age of 80 and over.
3. (a) Storks observe the practice of monogamy.
   (b) Storks are monogamous.
4. When an iguana is threatened, it uses its tail effectively as a whip.
5. Cats eat one-third of all the canned fish in the United States.

Exercise 4.5

Here are some possible rewrites; yours may differ.

1. Human beings can develop their physical senses to a much higher degree than most people realize.
2. Anyone can find enough examples from everyday life to determine that this is true.
3. For example, an experienced vintner can taste the amount of alcohol or acid in a particular wine to within one percent.
4. Expert color technicians can see differences between certain shades of red that are indistinguishable to the layperson.
5. Some professional bakers can measure the moisture content of bread dough to within two percent of accuracy just by its feel when they are kneading it.

Exercise 4.6

1. Zsa Zsa Gabor once said, "I'm a wonderful housekeeper. Every time I get a divorce, I keep the house."
2. In 1787, the United States minted a copper coin with a simple motto: "Mind Your business."
3. *The Outer Limits*, a science fiction TV series, always

opened with the same line: "There is nothing wrong with your set."

4. "Assassination is the extreme form of censorship," claimed George Bernard Shaw, the famous playwright.

5. indirect quote; no change

Chapter 5 Answer Key

Throughout this chapter, the sample combinations offered are not the only possible revisions. You may have come up with other good revisions.

Exercise 5.1

A. 1. Two football teams from King's Island, Alaska, were practicing before the 1938 New Year's Day Ice Bowl game.

   2. They had been practicing on a huge flat ice floe near their village.

   3. When they went out to practice on December 18, 1937, they couldn't find their practice field; gale-force winds had blown it away.

B. Traditionally, French boxers had kissed each other at the end of each bout, but that practice was officially banned by the French Boxing Federation in 1924.

C. 1. How slow can you go and still win?

   2. The slowest time for a winning racehorse was set during a steeplechase in 1945.

   3. The horse, which was named Never Mind II, refused a jump, so his jockey gave up and returned the horse to the paddock.

   4. When the jockey arrived at the paddock, he learned that all the other horses had either fallen or been disqualified.

   5. So he jumped on Never Mind II and rode him back onto the track.

   6. Never Mind II won the two-mile race, normally finished in 4 minutes, in 11 minutes and 28 seconds.

D. 1. Here's another odd bit of trivia from the world of horseracing.

   2. A jockey named Hayes dropped dead immediately after winning the first race of his career on June 4, 1923.

E. 1. The "New York Nine" and the Knickerbockers played the first official baseball game in the United States on June 19, 1846.

   2. During the game, a New York player started a long

187

and rich baseball tradition by swearing at the umpire.

3. The New York player, who was named Davis, was fined six cents for his outburst.

F. 1. Hockey is known for its violence, and most of it seems to be intentional.

2. But one hockey game, which was played on the junior amateur level in Quebec in 1930, was marked by a very unusual incident of unintentional violence.

3. A puck that was lined at the goalie, Able Goldberry, struck a pack of matches in his pocket, and his uniform caught on fire.

4. The fire was put out by players and spectators, but Able Goldberry was badly burned in the bizarre incident.

G. 1. During a basketball game between sophomores and seniors on March 16, 1937, at St. Peter's High School in Fairmount, Virginia, all of the players on one team, with the exception of Pat McGee, fouled out.

2. When all the others fouled out, the game was tied at 32 - 32 with four minutes left to play.

3. It didn't look good for McGee's team.

4. But McGee faced the five players on the opposing team, scored a goal, made a foul shot, defended his team's basket, and prevented his opponents from scoring.

5. The final score was 35 - 32: McGee had won the game for his team single-handedly.

H. 1. In 1958, Robert Legge, a 53-year-old Navy doctor, swam the 28.5-mile-long Panama Canal in 21 hours and 54 minutes.

2. During the swim, he encountered only two living creatures: a boa constrictor and an iguana.

3. At times, swells caused by heavy ship traffic made his progress difficult.

4. When he arrived at Balboa, he was greeted by several hundred well-wishers and a toll collector, who charged Legge 72 cents, the minimum fee for a one-ton vessel in ballast.

I. 1. In 1890, a best-of-seven postseason baseball series was played between New York of the National League and St. Louis of the American Association.

2. New York had won three games and St. Louis had won two when the St. Louis Browns won game

six to tie up the series at three games apiece.

3. After they evened up the series, the Browns stayed out all night celebrating, and the next day they claimed to be "too tuckered out" to take the field; as a consequence, the final game was canceled, and the best-of-seven series stands as "tied 3 - 3" in the record books today.

J. 1. In 1865, Louis Fox was playing pool against John Deery in Rochester, New York, for a $1,000 purse.

2. Louis Fox, a billiard champion, was enjoying a very comfortable lead when a fly suddenly landed on the cue ball.

3. The problem was how to get the fly to move without moving the cue ball.

4. Those who were present tried everything, but the fly would not budge, no matter what anyone did.

5. Fox was more than bugged by the presence of the fly; in fact, he became completely rattled.

6. Angry at miscuing and losing the match to Deery, he rushed out of the pool hall.

7. Several days later, his body was found floating in the river near the pool hall, and many people assumed that Fox committed suicide after his strange loss.

Exercise 5.2

A. 1. Several years ago, the editors of *Psychology Today* asked their readers if they remembered their dreams.

2. Of the more than 1,000 readers who responded, approximately 95 percent reported that they do remember some of their dreams, and about 68 percent claimed to have a recurring dream.

3. Two themes were represented most frequently in the recurring dreams: the experience of being chased and the sensation of falling.

4. The readers reported other recurring themes, including flying, appearing naked or almost naked in a public place, being unprepared to take a test, and returning to one's childhood home.

5. About 45 percent of the readers said that they sometimes dream about celebrities, usually sex symbols and rock stars.

6. After sex symbols and rock stars, people most often reported dreaming about politicians and historical

figures, such as Abraham Lincoln.

7. Lincoln himself put a lot of stock in dreams; in fact, he believed that one dream had forewarned him that he would be assassinated.

8. Of those who responded to the *Psychology Today* survey, 28 percent had seen themselves die in a dream; that sounds very ominous, but most experts say a dream of one's own death should not be at all frightening.

B. 1. Psychologist Ann Faraday, author of *The Dream Game,* says that a dream about one's death often indicates something far different from what you might expect.

2. She says it usually symbolizes the death of an obsolete self-image and signals an opportunity to move to a higher state of self-definition.

3. The interpretation of dreams in general is a highly controversial area.

4. Those who follow Sigmund Freud believe that dreams are the key to the unconscious.

5. Those who follow the thinking of Nobel laureate Francis Crick believe that dreams are a garbage disposal for the mind.

6. According to Crick, the function of dreams is to clear out useless information that interferes with rational thought and memory.

7. A third school of thought consists of psychologists who believe that dreams are important not in themselves, but only because people think they are important.

8. These psychologists believe that people give dreams their meaning, influence, and power.

Exercise 5.3

A. 1. *The People's Almanac #3,* by David Wallechinsky and Irving Wallace, includes a cautionary tale for anyone who has ever daydreamed about what it would be like to be a giant.

2. It's not a tall tale; it's the true story of Robert Wadlow, probably the tallest person who ever lived.

3. Wadlow, who was born in Alton, Illinois, on February 22, 1918, was a normal eight-and-a-half-pound baby boy.

4. The medical history of his family, in which there were no unusually tall members, was normal.

5. But he grew rapidly and steadily from his birth until his death.

6. At six months, he weighed 30 pounds, which is about double the weight of a normal baby at that age.

7. When he was weighed again at 18 months, a time when the average toddler weighs 24 or 25 pounds, Wadlow weighed 62 pounds.

8. He was five feet, four inches tall and 105 pounds when he underwent his first thorough examination at the age of 5.

9. Wearing clothes made for 17-year-olds, he started school when he was five and a half.

10. When he was measured again at the age of 8,he had reached a height of six feet, and his father, Robert Wadlow, Sr., started wearing hand-me-downs from his son.

B. 1. After Wadlow was diagnosed at age 12 with excessive pituitary gland secretion, careful records of his growth were kept at Washington University in St. Louis, Missouri.

2. He grew an average of three inches a year throughout his life; at his death on July 15, 1940, his height was eight feet, eleven inches.

3. His early death was not surprising.

4. Pituitary giants usually die before middle age because their organs outgrow the ability to function correctly.

5. Because physical coordination becomes difficult for a giant, he or she usually has many more accidents than a normal-sized person has.

6. A giant's accidents also tend to result in more serious injuries, which is compounded by the fact that a giant's body heals more slowly.

7. Wadlow in particular had more than his share of physical problems, beginning with surgery for a double hernia when he was 2 years old.

8. Everything he encountered in this world was on the wrong scale: school desks were too small, doorways were too low, beds were too short, and chairs were too tiny.

9. He had terrible problems with his feet.

10. Doctors advised Wadlow to walk as much as possible to strengthen his feet, but the walking damaged his arches even more severely.

11. For a while, he attended Shurtieff College with the hope of becoming a lawyer, but he had to drop out because it was too difficult for him to walk from classroom to classroom.

C. 1. Though Robert Wadlow's life was marked by tragedy, it wasn't completely tragic.

2. He was intelligent and charming, and he had good parents who tried to make his life as normal and as full as possible.

3. His boyhood days were filled with typical things: hobbies, sports, Boy Scouts, and books.

4. But his life was also filled with things that were not so typical.

5. The more unusual aspects of Wadlow's story started when he was discovered by the media at age 9.

6. It happened when the Associated Press came across a photograph and circulated it in newspapers all across the nation.

7. That's when Robert Wadlow became a public person.

8. From that time on, he had to deal with a steady stream of people: reporters, medical researchers, curiosity seekers, and entrepreneurs.

9. Theatrical agents who wanted his services made very attractive offers to pressure him to perform.

10. His parents rejected all opportunities to make money from his misfortune.

11. He did, however, make paid appearances for the Peters Shoe Company in St. Louis.

12. This endorsement arrangement was appropriate because Wadlow had to have specially made shoes; unfortunately, he often outgrew new shoes even before they were delivered.

13. Robert Wadlow also worked for a short time in 1937 for the Ringling Brothers Circus in New York and Boston, but there were strict conditions in his contract.

14. The conditions stated that he would make only three-minute appearances in the center ring in ordinary street clothes; he would not appear in the sideshow.

15. Wadlow occasionally made appearances for churches to raise funds for charities; he accepted no pay for these activities.

D 1. In 1936, Robert Wadlow had a visit from a small-town Missouri doctor who was studying giantism.

2. He happened to catch Wadlow on one of his relatively rare bad days.

3. The doctor later wrote an article about Wadlow for the *Journal of the American Medical Association* in which he described Wadlow as dull and surly.

4. According to The *People's Almanac #3*, this characterization is generally true of most pathological giants, but it was not true of Robert Wadlow, who was truly an exceptional human being.

5. The unflattering description in the medical journal hurt and disillusioned Wadlow for two reasons.

6. First, all his life he had put up with medical researchers who had invaded his privacy and taken up his time, and he had done so voluntarily and graciously.

7. Second, the article was based on the quick impressions the doctor had made after a visit of less than an hour.

8. Wadlow and his family wanted his character vindicated, so they took legal action against the doctor and the American Medical Association (AMA).

9. The AMA strongly defended the doctor, so the litigation dragged on and on and was not resolved when Wadlow died at the age of 22.

10. Partly as a result of this episode, Wadlow stipulated that after his death he wanted his body to be kept out of the hands of medical researchers.

11. In accordance with his wishes, there was no examination of his body after his death.

12. He was buried in a custom-built 10-foot-long casket, which was placed in an almost impregnable tomb in his hometown.

13. More than 46,000 people came to the funeral home in Alton, Illinois, to pay their last respects to Robert Wadlow.

Better Sentence-Writing

A. 1. Judith Rodin, who teaches psychology at Yale University, has been involved in important studies on a number of topics, including bystander intervention, learned helplessness, obesity, and aging.

2. She is interested in relationships in general, but she is especially interested in the relationship between the mind and the body and the relationship between biology and environment.

3. Older people, in particular, have benefitted from Rodin's research.

4. In fact, it's been said that it's not easy for her to find places in Connecticut where she can continue to study the problems of older people in nursing homes because the state's nursing homes have improved so much as a result of her work.

5. At one point in her career, Rodin, along with psychologist Ellen Langer, conducted a fascinating study on perceived choice among residents of nursing homes, and this study was described in *Psychology Today*.

6. Perceived choice is the amount of control that a person believes he or she has over events.

7. On the basis of laboratory studies, Rodin already knew that the degree to which people feel they can exert control in important areas of their lives influences three things: their happiness, their ability to perform, and their sense of well-being.

B. 1. Judith Rodin and Ellen Langer wanted to investigate perceived choice or control in a real-life setting, so they chose a nursing home.

2. They were especially interested in the relationship between the degree of control that the nursing home residents thought they had and the residents' health and happiness.

3. Rodin and Langer believed that improvements in well-being would be quite obvious among the sick and frail residents of a nursing home once they were given increased control.

4. It would be difficult to show the positive benefits of an increased sense of control in people who were younger and healthier

because, in that group, any benefits would more likely be in the form of prevention rather than improvement.

5. The results of the study were indeed dramatic.

6. Nursing home residents in the study were given new choices, many of which seemed quite trivial, in areas in which they previously had no choice.

7. For example, residents were allowed to choose when they could see a movie and how to arrange their rooms.

C. 1. The choices may have been trivial, but the results were not.

2. Using a variety of methods of measurement, the researchers discovered that the residents' new sense of control had a number of effects: the residents' health and overall mental state improved, and dropped the death rate at the nursing home.

3. Why would having new choices in trivial areas of life produce such profound effects?

4. Rodin explains that the choices seem trivial only to people who have a broad range of choices in their lives; to those who have

little or no choice, any choice at all has a great impact.

5. A sense of control or perceived choice created a profound psychological state in which the residents felt better about themselves.

6. They felt a sense of power, which caused them to respond more positively to family members, other residents, and nurses and doctors. In turn, everyone in their lives responded more positively toward them.

7. Choosing when to see a movie or where to put a picture on a wall might seem trivial, but Rodin says that small bit of control can have an energizing effect on every aspect of an older person's life.

Exercise 5.5

A. 1. Mabel Keaton Staupers, a fast-talking, energetic black woman, was one of the outstanding women of the twentieth century.

2. Almost single-handedly, she broke a link in a chain, a chain that had kept many black women from using their talents and skills and had denied them

their full rights as American citizens.

3. A classic David and Goliath tale, her fascinating and inspiring story is told in *Black Leaders of the Twentieth Century.*

4. It is the story of a battle between one woman, the executive secretary of the National Association of Colored Graduate Nurses (NACGN), and two branches of the military, the U.S. Army and the Navy.

5. Mabel K. Staupers's accomplishment must be viewed within the context of a certain period in American history if it is to be fully appreciated.

6. It was around the time that the United States entered into World War II, and for many reasons, including the anti-Nazi mood of the nation, American blacks recently had become much less accepting of the racial status quo.

7. For many blacks, their unequal treatment in their own country was highlighted in an ironic way by America's opposition to Nazi Germany.

8. In opposing the philosophy and actions of Germany's

Nazis, the U.S. government, many members of the press, and the public in general did a lot of talking about the ideals upon which America had been founded.

9. They contrasted Germany to an America that was pure in the realization of its democratic ideals andjust in its treatment of people of different religious, ethnic, and racial backgrounds.

10. Such statements about this country struck some Americans, both blacks and whites, as hypocritical and ironic.

11. Summing up the situation, Walter White wrote, "World War II has immeasurably magnified the Negro's awareness of the disparity between the American profession and practice of democracy."

B. 1. It was during this time that Mabel K. Staupers used patience, persistence, and a great deal of political savvy to begin her long fight for the rights of black nurses.

2. Staupers, who was born in Barbados, West Indies, in 1890, came to New York with her parents in 1903.

3. After graduating from Freedmen's Hospital School

of Nursing in Washington,
D.C., in 1917, she began
her career as a private
nurse in New York City.

4. She played an important
role in establishing the
Booker T. Washington
Sanatorium in Harlem,
which was the first facility
in the area where black
doctors could treat
patients.

5. Then she worked for 12
years as the executive
secretary for the Harlem
Committee of the New York
Tuberculosis and Health
Association.

6. Finally in 1934, Staupers
was appointed executive
secretary of the NACGN,
and in this position, she
had one goal: to help black
nurses become fully inte-
grated into the mainstream
of American health care.

7. Then the United States
entered World War II in
1941.

8. Because the war created a
great demand for nurses to
care for the wounded,
Mabel K. Staupers had a
perfect opportunity to
realize her goal.

9. That demand could result
in the acceptance of black
nurses into the Army and
Navy Nurse Corps, which
would be the vehicle for the
full inclusion of blacks into
the profession of nursing in
America.

C. 1. Staupers knew that black
nurses had suffered great
discrimination in World
War I, and she vowed that
would not happen again.

2. So Staupers fought her
own battle on various
fronts throughout the years
of the American war effort.

3. First, she fought the
exclusion of black women
from the Army and Navy
Nurse Corps.

4. Later, when the Army
established a quota system
for black nurses, she fought
the quota system because it
implied that black nurses
were inferior to other
nurses.

5. At one point, she also
fought the military's policy
of having black nurses care
for black soldiers and no
others.

6. The Army finally assigned
black nurses to care for
white soldiers, but only
white soldiers who were
German prisoners of war,
not American, so she
fought that practice, too.

D. 1. These were tough battles,
but Staupers eventually
found a powerful ally in
First Lady Eleanor
Roosevelt.

2. Eleanor Roosevelt began lobbying for black nurses.

3. She talked to Norman T. Kirk, surgeon general of the U.S. Army, W.J.C. Agnew, a rear admiral in the U.S. Navy, and Franklin D. Roosevelt, her husband.

4. Meanwhile, Staupers staged a public confrontation with Norman T. Kirk that received a good deal of press coverage.

5. In a speech at the Hotel Pierre in New York, Kirk described the dire shortage of nurses in the Army and predicted that a draft for nurses might be necessary.

6. Staupers was in Kirk's audience of about 300 people, which included nurses, politicians, and private citizens.

7. She rose to her feet and asked the surgeon general, "If nurses are needed so desperately, why isn't the Army using colored nurses?"

8. She explained to the audience that, while there were 9,000 black registered nurses in the United States, the Army had taken 247 and the Navy had taken none.

9. According to newspaper reports, Kirk was visibly uncomfortable and didn't have much of an answer for Staupers.

E. 1. At about the same time, President Roosevelt announced in a radio address on January 6, 1945, that he wanted to amend the Selective Service Act of 1940 so that nurses could be drafted.

2. The public reaction was tremendous; the irony of calling for a general draft while at the same time discriminating against black nurses was obvious to almost everyone.

3. Staupers showed a lot of political savvy in the way she handled the public's dissatisfaction with the plans of the top brass.

4. She gave speeches, issued press releases, and urged people to send telegrams to President Roosevelt.

5. The groups that sent messages of protest to the White House included the National Association for the Advancement of Colored People (NAACP), the Congress of Industrial Organizations, the American Federation of Labor, the United Council of Church Women, the

Catholic Interracial Council, the Alpha Kappa Alpha Sorority, and the New York Citizens' Committee of the Upper West Side.

6. The great wave of public protest caused the Army, the Navy, and the War Department to drop the policies of exclusion, segregation, and quota systems for black nurses.

7. A few weeks later, Phyllis Dailey was the first black woman to break the color barrier in the U.S. Navy Nurse Corps.

8. The Army also began to accept black nurses with no restrictions.

9. Most of the credit goes to one woman alone: Mabel K. Staupers.

Chapter 6 Answer Key

Exercise 6.1

1. a carpenter builds
   carpenters build

2. one star shines
   all the stars shine

3. the golfer putts
   golfers putt

4. roses grow
   a rose grows

5. the chimneys smoke
   the chimney smokes

6. a pitcher pitches
   pitchers pitch

7. one loaf rises
   the loaves rise

8. bombs explode
   a bomb explodes

9. the popsicle melts
   popsicles melt

10. last-minute shoppers rush
    a last-minute shopper rushes

Exercise 6.2

1. the article explains
   the articles explain

2. one baby cries
   all the babies cry

3. one player wins
   four players win

4. the team performs
   the teams perform

5. the ink spots dry
   the ink spot dries

6. the soldiers march
   a soldier marches

7. the telephone rings
   telephones ring

8. ideas form
   an idea forms

9. chickens hatch
   a chicken hatches

10. a peacemaker pacifies
    peacemakers pacify

Exercise 6.3

1. movie has
   movies have

2. attitude is
   attitudes are
3. carriers were
   carrier was
4. pretzels are
   pretzel is
5. fingernail was
   fingernails were

Exercise 6.4

Note: The subject of each clause is itaticized here.

1. *pounds* are; *intake* was; *Forecasters* say; *increases* are; *Meat and fruit* appear
2. *term* is
3. *fan* cares; *names* were
4. *habits* begin
5. *Final Payments and The Company of Women* are; *Men and Angels* is

Exercise 6.5

Note: The subject of each clause is italicized here.

1. *One* ends; *This* happens; *owner* plunks ... forces; *one* shares
2. *nuts* stay; *they* remain; *pecans and Brazil nuts* keep; *you* store
3. *Moonbeams* are ... take
4. *life span* depends; *moisture* is; *moisture and oil* affect; *cards* are; *condition* is; *deck* lasts;

pack has; *cards* show; *they* slow; *they* are
5. *series* is; *length* is; *earthquakes* have; *one* was

Exercise 6.6

1. murdered; *past*
2. was introduced; vp
3. damaged; adj
4. distinguished; adj
5. captured; *past*
6. admired; adj
7. was established; vp
8. are experienced; vp
9. is supposed; vp
10. showed; *past*

Exercise 6.7

1. no change
2. change *would always be* to *has always been* or *was always*
3. no change
4. change *could have been* to *had been* or *were*
5. change *contained* to *contain*
6. change *had* to *have;* change *offered* to *offer*
7. omit *would* or change *would* to *can;* change *would need* to *need* or *will need*
8. no change
9. change *would also be* to *are also*
10. no change

200

11. change *had* to *has;* change
    would have to *has;* change
    were to *are*
12. no change
13. no change

Exercise 6.8

1. one librarian's duties
   two librarians' duties
2. the child's excitement
   the children's excitement
3. the dancer's shoes
   both dancers' shoes
4. one boy's pet chameleon
   three boys' pet chameleons
5. the family's history
   the two families' histories
6. the woman's schedule
   the women's schedules
7. the poet's images
   many poets' images
8. one rabbit's carrots
   all the rabbits' carrots
9. one drummer's performance
   the drummers' performance
10. the businessman's trips
    the businessmen's trips

Exercise 6.9

1. the mayor's priorities
2. the pilots' training
3. Jerry Seinfeld's comic talents
4. the coaches' game plan
5. the vendor's ice-cream
   sandwiches

6. the babies' toys
7. the friends' agreement
8. Whitney Houston's voice
9. Rob Morrow's role in
   Northern Exposure
10. the clowns' role in the circus

Exercise 6.10

1. the National Restaurant
   Association's question
2. The research organization's
   national survey; Americans'
   top five restaurant food
   choices
3. the nation's cafes and
   restaurants
4. restaurant diners' top menu
   choices
5. A typical New Yorker's order
6. people's favorites
7. anyone's guess; North
   Dakotans' restaurant
   preferences
8. residents' first loves
9. a restaurant's menu
10. restaurant customers' tastes

Exercise 6.11

1. A parent's greatest fear
2. no apostrophe needed
3. women's concerns; the
   couple's list
4. Hechinger's how-to book
5. many children's training

Better Sentence-Writing

Exercise 6.12

1. it was; *ante.* = Medal of Honor
2. it; *ante.* = the Hurley Machine Company
3. They were; *ante.* = Nikon cameras
4. It has, its; *ante.* = Salvation Army
5. he was; *ante.* = Neanderthal man
6. his; *ante.* = neither Gary Player nor his son
7. their; *ante.* = Ostrich eggs it; *ante.* = one
8. it; *ante.* = the orchestra
9. them; *ante.* = Paper straws
10. (a) its, its; *ante.* = empire
    (b) they, their; *ante.* = people

Exercise 6.13

1. it was; *ante.* = stamp
2. they will; *ante.* rulers it expires; *ante.* = a lease
3. its; *ante.* = U.S. Football League
4. its; *ante.* = Fairy Investigation Society
5. their; *ante.* = tarantulas

Exercise 6.14

1. him
2. she
3. them
4. I
5. we
6. her
7. they
8. me
9. he
10. me

Exercise 6.15

1. than; too
2. principal; than; there
3. to; through
4. principle; course; effect; number; to; its
5. who's; than; you're; your; to
6. finely; two; than
7. finally; threw; passed; than; conscience
8. accept; Their
9. number; than
10. It's; there
11. you're; too; have; Its; number
12. course; there; affect; to
13. too; here; two
14. number; bear; too
15. there; affect; an; to; course; conscience; too

Exercise 6.16

1. New York Museum of Modern Art; French artist Henri Matisse's *Le Bateau*
2. Chaucer; "Love is blind,"; William Shakespeare

3. Lincoln Memorial;
   Washington, D.C.

4. Hemingway; American; *The Sun Also Rises; A Farewell to Arms; For Whom the Bell Tolls; The Old Man and the Sea;* Fridays

5. *Sudden Impact;* Clint Eastwood; "Make my day."

6. Volkswagen Beetle

7. Russian

8. President Jimmy Carter

9. West; Cheyenne, Wyoming; "Hell on Wheels."

10. John Lindsay; New York City; *Rosebud*

Sources

The examples and exercises in *Better Sentence-Writing In 30 Minutes a Day* were drawn from the following sources. Books are arranged alphabetically by title; magazine and newspaper articles are arranged alphabetically by article title.

Books

The American Heritage Dictionary of the English Language, ed. William Morris, American Heritage Publishing Co., Inc., and Houghton Mifflin Company, New York, 1975.

The Best by Peter Passell and Leonard Ross, Farrar, Straus and Giroux, New York, 1974.

Black Leaders of the Twentieth Century, University of Illinois Press, Urbana, Illinois, 1982.

The Book of Firsts by Patrick Robertson, Bramhall House, Crown Publishers, Inc., New York, 1982.

The Book of Lists #3 by Amy Wallace, David Wallechinsky, and Irving Wallace, William Morrow and Company, Inc., New York, 1983.

Can Elephants Swim? by Robert M. Jones, Time-Life Books, New York, 1969.

Cross Your Fingers, Spit in Your Hat by Alvin Schwartz and Glen Rounds, J.B. Lippincott Company, Philadelphia and New York, 1974.

The Dance Encyclopedia by Anatole Chujoy and P.W. Manchester, Simon and Schuster, New York, 1967.

Deep Song: The Dance Story of Martha Graham by Ernestine Stodelle, Schirmer Books, New York, 1984.

Better Sentence-Writing

Dick Clark's The First 25 Years of Rock & Roll by Michael Uslan and Bruce Solomon, Delacorte Press, New York, 1981.

Encyclopaedia Britannica, Volumes 7 and 22, Encyclopaedia Britannica, Inc., William Benton, Publisher, Chicago, 1963.

The Encyclopedia of Sports by Frank G. Menke, A. S. Barnes and Company, New York, 1960.

From Slavery to Freedom: A History of Negro Americans, 4th ed., by John Hope Franklin, Alfred A. Knopf, New York, 1974.

The Great American Sports Book by George Gipe, A Dolphin Book, Doubleday & Company, Inc., Garden City, New York, 1978.

The Healing Heart by Norman Cousins, W. W. Norton & Company, New York, 1983.

The Heart of Hollywood by Bob Thomas, Price/Stern/Sloan Publishers, Inc., Los Angeles, California, 1971.

How to Raise a Street-Smart Child by Grace Hechinger, Facts On File Publications, New York, 1984.

Incredible Animals, A to Z, National Wildlife Federation, 1985.

Joan Embery's Collection of Amazing Animal Facts by Joan Embery with Ed Lucaire, Delacorte Press, New York, 1983.

Knock on Wood: An Encyclopedia of Talismans, Charms, Superstitions & Symbols, Carole Potter, Beaufort Books, Inc., New York, 1983.

Life-spans, Or, How Long Things Last by Frank Kendig and Richard Hutton, Holt, Rinehart and Winston, New York, 1979.

Linden Hills by Gloria Naylor, Ticknor & Fields, New York, 1985.

The Misunderstood Child by Larry B. Silver, McGraw-Hill Book Company, New York, 1984.

More FYI, For Your Information, ed. Nat Brandt, M. Evans and Company, Inc., New York, 1983.

The People's Almanac #2 by David Wallechinsky and Irving Wallace, Bantam Books, New York, 1978.

The People's Almanac #3 by David Wallechinsky and Irving Wallace, Bantam Books, New York, 1981

Pictorial History of American Sports by John Durant and Otto Bettmann, A. S. Barnes and Company, New York, 1952.

The Presidents, Tidbits & Trivia by Sid Frank and Arden Davis Melick, Greenwich House, a division of Arlington House, Inc., distributed by Crown Publishers, Inc., New York, 1984.

The Quintessential Quiz Book by Norman G. Hickman, St. Martin's Press, New York, 1979.

Race Matters by Cornel West, Beacon Press, Boston, 1993.

The Rolling Stone Encyclopedia of Rock & Roll, eds. Jon Pareles and Patricia Romanowski, Rolling Stone Press/Summit Books, New York, 1983.

The Rule Book by Stephen M. Kirschner, Barry J. Pavelec, and Jeffrey Feinman, A Dolphin Book, Doubleday & Company, Inc., Garden City, New York, 1979.

Speaker's Treasury of Anecdotes About the Famous by James C. Humes, Harper & Row, Publishers, Inc., New York, 1978.

Sources

Stay Tuned, A Concise History of American Broadcasting by Christopher H. Sterling and John M. Kittros, Wadsworth Publishing Co., Belmont, California, 1978.

This Day in Sports by John G. Fetros, Newton K. Gregg, Publisher, Novato, California, 1974.

Van Gogh by Gerald E. Finley, Tudor Publishing Company, New York, 1966.

The Westerners by Dee Brown, Holt, Rinehart and Winston, New York, 1974.

Your Five-Year-Old, Sunny, and Serene by Louise Bates Ames and Frances L. Ilg, A Delta Book, Dell Publishing Co., Inc., 1979.

Magazine and Newspaper Articles

"A Cutthroat Business," by Philip Jacobson, *Connoisseur*, December 1994.

"A Sense of Control," by Elizabeth Hall, *Psychology Today*, December 1984.

"A very special crystal: Mystique of diamonds still endures," by Dennis R. Getto, *The Milwaukee Journal*, April 24, 1985.

"After 73 Years, a Titanic Find," *Time*, September 16, 1985.

"An aching America," UPI, *The Milwaukee Journal*, October 22, 1985.

"An Ancient 'Nuclear Winter,'" by Sharon Begley, *Newsweek*, October 14, 1985.

"Bakelite Envy, Depression-Era Plastic Costume Jewelry Has Become a Hot Item," by Andrea DiNoto, *Connoisseur*, July 1985.

"Coffee trivia," *The Milwaukee Journal*, April 24, 1985.

"Death of an American Icon," by Jack Kroll, *Newsweek*, August 23, 1982.

"Facing up to feelings: Your expressions may trigger physical reactions," Los Angeles Times service, *The Milwaukee Journal*, June 18, 1985.

"Ferrets fancied by city dwellers," by Caroline Nichols, *Milwaukee Sentinel*, October 7, 1985.

"Fish—For Health," *Vogue*, July 1985.

"Following in the footsteps of Rachel Carson," by Robert W. Smith, *USA Today*, April 5, 1985.

"For every region, a special food," by Dan Sperling, *USA Today*, October 8, 1985.

"Getting there without motion sickness," by Cynthia Dennis, *The Milwaukee Journal*, April 29, 1985.

"Houses from Sears," by Nelson Groffman, *Country Living*, June 1984.

"Little Swamis," by Claire Warga, *Psychology Today*, January 1985.

"Looking for Mr. Good Bear," *Newsweek*, December 24, 1984.

"Mabel K. Staupers and the Integration of Black Nurses into the Armed Forces," by Darlene Clark Hine, in *Black Leaders of the Twentieth Century*, eds. John Hope Franklin and August Meier, University of Illinois Press, Urbana, Illinois, 1982.

207

Better Sentence-Writing

"Manhattan Serenade," by David Ansen, *Newsweek,* February 3, 1986.
"Name Calling," by Harris Dienstfrey, *Psychology Today,* January 1983.
"New Bodies For Sale," *Newsweek,* May 27, 1985.
"Nuclear Winter and Carbon Dioxide," by John Maddox, *Nature,* December 13, 1984.
"Nutty pets often the owner's fault." UPI. *The Milwaukee Sentinel,* April 26, 1985.
"Overachievers—When Toil Gets Them in Trouble," *Vogue,* May 1985.
"Pets can pose problems." UPI, *The Milwaukee Journal,* June 9, 1985.
"Pulitzer winner tapped as U.S. poet laureate," AP, *The Ann Arbor News,* May 19, 1993.
"Rah, rah, rah: As spirit grows, so do souvenir sales," UPI, *The Milwaukee Journal,* April 11, 1985.
"Remember Them?" Jacquelyn Mitchard, *The Milwaukee Journal,* March 17, 1985.
"Ruth Gordon: her life and work had 'this zing,'" by Michael Gordon, Washington Post Service, *The Milwaukee Journal,* August 31, 1985.
"The Secret Payoff of Hypochondria," *Vogue,* August 1983.
"So THAT'S what it was!" by Michael Bauman, *The Milwaukee Journal,* October 2, 1985.
"Strong, special bond sustains sisters through life," by Barbara Bisantz Raymond, *USA Today,* August 8, 1983.
"They're still making 501 jeans the old-fashioned way," *The Milwaukee Journal,* April 17, 1985.
"Thieves like popular cars, too," *The Milwaukee Journal,* May 4, 1985.
"Titanic: The questions remain," Duane Valentry, copyright 1985 Duane Valentry, News America Syndicate, *The Milwaukee Journal,* April 15, 1985.
"To Sleep, Perchance to Dream," by Elizabeth Stark, *Psychology Today,* October 1984.
"The US trivia team has a quiz for you," by Gary C. Rummler, *The Milwaukee Journal,* June 12, 1985.
"Washington married into money," AP, *The Milwaukee Journal,* April 29, 1985.
"What Makes a Top Executive?" by Morgan W. McCall, Jr., and Michael M. Lombardo, *Psychology Today,* February 1983.
"What's black and orange and scary?" by Tony Staffieri, *The Milwaukee Journal,* October 17, 1985.
"Will the Real Impostor Please Stand Up?" by Jeff Meer, *Psychology Today,* April 1985.

Index

A

Action verbs, 2
Adjectives, 20
Adjective pairs, 67
Adjective phrases, 24
Adverb phrase, 24
Adverbs, 21-22
"And", 132f
Antecedents, 155ff
Apostrophes, 148-154
Appositives, 22-23

B

"Being", 49

C

Can/could, 146
Clauses, 1-9, 14-15, 30,
    31ff, 47-48, 73-74
Colons, 78-81
Combining
    sentences, 29-52
Comma(s), 53-70

Comma splices, 41ff
Complex
    sentences, 32-34, 53ff
Compound
    sentences, 29-31, 53ff
Conjunctions, 31ff
Contractions, 154
Coordinating
    conjunctions, 31
Cutoff modifier, 50-51

D

Dangling modifiers, 87ff
Delayed subject, 133-134
Dependent clauses, 32ff,
    47-48
Direct objects, 5ff
Direction words, 25

E

"-ed" endings, 137-142
Embedded
    sentences, 35-40, 56-61
Embedding, 49-50